HONOUR A
A Histoı

MW01100601

The Royal Society of Canada is the country's oldest national organization dedicated to the encouragement of the humanities and sciences and the recognition of conspicuous merit. Men and women elected to membership (FRSC) have included virtually every major figure, and many secondary ones, in Canadian scientific and literary history. An institution in which many currents converged and interacted, the society has mirrored in microcosm the salient themes in the country's intellectual development, not least with respect to French-English relations. In this critical history of the Royal Society, Carl Berger observes that its twin objectives of honouring intellectual achievement and promoting scholarship proved to be not entirely compatible.

The book opens with an account of the origins, organization, and early lobbying efforts of the society. Berger surveys the important role of the society's *Transactions* in publishing research in history, ethnology, and the natural and physical sciences. He finds that, over the years, and in contrast to the often-considerable efforts and achievements of its individual fellows, the institutional significance of the Royal Society has generally amounted to something less that the sum of its parts. While the society has always encouraged and sometimes nurtured a range of national institutions, including the country's national archives, library, art gallery, and museum, as well as others in the sciences (such as the National Research Council) and the arts (for example, the Canada Council), Berger points out that these accomplishments often came in spite of ineffective or indecisive support from the society; rather, they emerged through the initiatives and concern of individual members.

CARL BERGER is a professor in the Department of History at the University of Toronto. He is author of *The Writing of Canadian History: Aspects of English-Canadian Historical Writing, 1900–1970* and *The Sense of Power: Studies in the Ideas of Canadian Imperialism, 1867–1914.*

CARL BERGER

Honour and the Search for Influence: A History of the Royal Society of Canada

UNIVERSITY OF TORONTO PRESS
Toronto Buffalo London

Printed in Canada

ISBN 0-8020-0794-5 (cloth)
ISBN 0-8020-7153-8 (paper)

Printed on acid-free paper

Canadian Cataloguing in Publication Data

Berger, Carl, 1939–
Honour and the search for influence :
A history of the Royal Society of Canada

Includes bibliographical references and index.
ISBN 0-8020-0794-5 (bound)
ISBN 0-8020-7153-8 (pbk.)

1. Royal Society of Canada – History.   I. Title.

AS42.R67B47 1996   061'.1   C95-932964-1

This book has been published
with the help of a grant from the
Humanities and Social Sciences Federation
of Canada, using funds provided by the
Social Sciences and Humanities Research Council of Canada.

University of Toronto Press acknowledges the
financial assistance to its publishing program of the
Canada Council and the Ontario Arts Council.

FOR LAUREL

Contents

Preface

The Royal Society of Canada is the country's oldest national organization of intellectuals dedicated to the encouragement of the humanities and sciences and the recognition of conspicuous merit. Founded under vice-regal auspices fifteen years after Confederation, the society brought together geologists and poets and French and English historians into a federation that was of considerable importance in Canadian intellectual life in the late Victorian age. The society has included among its elected members virtually every major figure, and many secondary ones, in Canadian scientific and literary history. The society has been devoted both to honouring intellectual achievement and to promoting scholarship. These twin objectives have proved to be not entirely compatible, and this fact alone would make its experience of more than passing curiosity.

The history of the Royal Society is of much broader significance, for the society has been a national institution in which many currents have converged and interacted, and it has mirrored in microcosm the salient themes in the country's intellectual development. It has encompassed scientists and humanists, and its history reveals both the interplay between them and the friction attendant on the rise to dominance of the scientific enterprise. It has brought French and English into contact, and its experience illustrates accommodations that bore an uncanny resemblance

x   Preface

to their interaction on the larger, national stage. No less instructive was the emergence of the 'social sciences' and their struggle for recognition within an organization in which defenders of the older, classical and literary traditions were entrenched.

The experience of this institution reflects as well the gradual displacement of people who were scholars by avocation – judges who wrote history, or clergymen who added to the knowledge of natural history – by academics with their own conventions and outlooks. The latter tended to look on their predecessors as dilettantes and earnestly promoted specialization to the point of fragmentation and isolation. By the mid-twentieth century the Royal Society justified itself, at least in part, as an organization that aimed at bringing specialists in many fields into contact with one another. That it survived its first half-century is a puzzle that alerts us to the unappreciated role of inertia and vanity in the persistence of institutions.

The following pages, then, are intended to highlight these general motifs in the interplay of the institution, with its many permutations, and the changing environment in which it evolved.[1]

I want to thank several individuals who have encouraged and helped me in this study: Judge Jules Deschênes and Michael Dence, who were, respectively, president and executive director of the Royal Society of Canada when the project was initiated in 1990; Andrée Désilets, Ian Ross Robertson, and Don Smith; Ramsay Cook and Brian McKillop, who gave me constructive reactions to the manuscript; and, above all, Laurel MacDowell, to whom this book is dedicated, for unstinting support. As usual, it has been a pleasure to work with Gerald Hallowell, Robert Ferguson, and John Parry of the University of Toronto Press.

CARL BERGER

The Royal Society shortly will hold
Its annual meeting, as we have been told;
And as I'm a member, it's time to prepare
Of the honour and glory to claim a due share.

I'm down for a paper – a paper on what?
Two ideas on the subject are more than I've got.
But who much attention on such things bestows?
At the Royal Society everything goes.

From 'Preparing for the Royal Society,'
Grip, 36, no. 22 (30 May 1891), 348, quoted in
Ramsay Cook, 'Neglected Pine Blasters,'
Canadian Literature, 81 (Summer 1979), 105–6

HONOUR AND THE SEARCH
FOR INFLUENCE: A HISTORY OF
THE ROYAL SOCIETY OF CANADA

1

Origins and Early Character, 1882–1914

The formation of the Royal Society of Canada was initiated by the Scottish nobleman the Marquess of Lorne, governor general of Canada from 1878 to 1883, as part of his personal campaign to promote Canadian cultural institutions. Lorne was married to Princess Louise, the fourth daughter of Queen Victoria, and his appointment was calculated to revive an appreciation of the imperial connection. Lorne's marriage was troubled (historians have guessed that he was gay),[1] and his political functions were quite limited: it was in the intellectual realm that his personal tastes matched his vice-regal role. Lorne was an aesthete who painted, wrote poetry, and collected natural history specimens and Indian artefacts, and he knew many Canadian painters, writers, and scientists. In 1880, after consultations with art associations in Toronto and Montreal, he launched the Royal Academy of Art; in June 1881 he proposed the creation of a literary and scientific society, and his resolve was made firmer when, during the summer on a trip to the Canadian northwest, he learned that the Smithsonian Institution of Washington, DC, had collected ethnological specimens in the area. Late in 1881 Lorne conferred with a broad cross-section of Canadian educators, including Principal William Dawson of McGill University in Montreal and Pierre Chauveau, who had been superintendent of public instruction in Canada

East and premier of Quebec. Rev. George M. Grant of Queen's University in Kingston and Daniel Wilson, president of University College, Toronto, were consulted, and both were very sceptical about including a literary component in the proposed society. The group of advisers also included men of letters such as John George Bourinot, clerk of the House of Commons; and Narcisse-Henri-Edouard Faucher de Saint-Maurice; and scientists such as Alfred R.C. Selwyn, director of the Geological Survey of Canada, and the botanist George Lawson of Dalhousie University in Halifax. Late in December 1881 some of these people met in Dawson's home, drafted a provisional constitution, and prepared – with some difficulty – a list of 60 (later 80) prospective members.

Though Lorne launched the society, it was not created in a vacuum. There was a mood of optimism about Canada's prospects generally in the early 1880s and a measured hopefulness about its intellectual possibilities. In 1881, Bourinot had issued a survey of the intellectual development of the Canadian people, which conveyed a reassuring sense of modest but solid progress gauged by increasing enrolments in colleges and universities, numbers in the learned professions, and the growth of newspapers.[2] Bourinot offered an encyclopaedic coverage of the expansion of 'native literature' in French and English, and his essay was in fact a handy checklist of prospective candidates for at least the literary part of the society that Lorne had in mind. He also noticed as an encouraging sign the recent appearance of such important books by Canadians as Alpheus Todd's *Parliamentary Government in the British Colonies* (1880), John Charles Dent's *The Last Forty Years: Canada since the Union of 1841* (1881), and Benjamin Sulte's eight-volume *Histoire des Canadiens-français*, which began to appear in 1882. In 1880 the poet Louis Fréchette had received the Prix Montyon from the Académie française. In 1882 the most ambitious publishing undertaking of the century was begun: *Picturesque Canada*, compiled by

G.M. Grant and the painter Lucius O'Brien. Issued in instalments over two years, the venture secured 20,000 subscribers.

A similar impression of heightened intellectual activity was conveyed in Henry J. Morgan's annual register, which covered scientific news fully. Bourinot had mentioned science only incidentally as part of his account of the life of the mind, apart from noting Dawson's study of Acadian geology and efforts to reconcile science and scripture. Other observers, however, believed that it was in the sciences, thanks mainly to the work of the Geological Survey since 1842, that Canadians had made their mark abroad. The survey moved its offices and museum from Montreal to Ottawa in 1881: readers of Morgan's chronicle were informed in detail of the survey's explorations as well as of the efforts of the natural history societies in the country's larger centres. Lorne laid the cornerstone of the Peter Redpath Museum in Montreal, which was intended to open on the occasion of the 1882 meeting of the American Association for the Advancement of Science – of which Dawson was president. In 1882 the governor general was reported to be corresponding with the presidents of the Royal Society of London and the British Association for the Advancement of Science regarding visits to Canada.[3]

The creation of the Royal Society of Canada expressed a sense of the quickening movement in the new country's intellectual life; it also represented a striving for cohesion, a bringing together of dispersed individuals and institutions. It was a logical extension of the political consolidation of the colonies. In explaining the society's Act of Incorporation to the Commons in 1883, Joseph Tassé made the parallel directly: 'After having abolished the Custom House barriers between the provinces, after having concluded a political union between them ... it was desirable that this political federation should be crowned with an intellectual, a scientific and literary federation.'[4]

The founders of the society were aware of models and

precedents for national academies dating from seven-teenth-century Europe. They eschewed the examples of the British Association for the Advancement of Science and its American counterpart, which were open to every-one with an interest in science, and determined that their organization would be honorary, like the Royal Society of London and the Institut français, whose memberships were limited to scholars of renown. Lorne had little patience with popular assemblages in which fools could not be kept in their places, and Dawson was emphatic on the point that membership in the Canadian body should be limited to producers and not include consumers. It was assumed that the very existence of such distinctions would provide an incentive for promise to grow, by application, into achievement. Membership was to be a counterpart to the titles of honour bestowed by the crown on deserving sol-diers and statesmen in recognition of exceptional service to the state. (Some charter members, or charter fellows, of the society were acutely conscious of such honours: Faucher de Saint-Maurice had an obsession with decora-tions that bordered on the unseemly; George Stewart, edi-tor of Quebec City's *Daily Chronicle*, who collected uni-versity degrees, asked G.M. Grant point blank for one from Queen's;[5] and Daniel Wilson, who was offered a knighthood at the rank of knight bachelor, at first indig-nantly refused it because politicians were honoured with higher orders and he took this offer as a slight to all men of letters and science.)

It was this principle of selectivity that called down on the heads of the founders charges of cliquishness. The historian and controversialist Goldwin Smith, who had little faith in most Canadian institutions and aspirations, wrote that the 'selection of members inevitably involved invidious preferences and rejections which were not rati-fied by public opinion, while anything like exclusiveness is repelled, and rightly repelled, by the spirit of Canadian society.'[6] Edward Blake, leader of the Liberal opposition

in the Commons when the society's government grant
was discussed (sandwiched between the problem of the
Acadia Power Company and immigrant sheds, roads, and
bridges in Regina), said that he would have more confi-
dence in the vitality of an institution that sought support
mainly from those interested in its objects than in one that
began 'by proposing that the public should become its
dry nurse.' The combination of selective, self-perpetuat-
ing membership and dependence on public funds seemed
especially repugnant to old liberals. The *Week* in 1890 went
so far as to call the statute a 'kind of un-Canadian class
legislation.'[7] Bourinot, who became secretary of the new
body, endured special censure at the hands of the erratic
journalist Nicholas Flood Davin, author of a history of the
Irish in Canada, who ridiculed his shortcomings as a prose
writer, a point expanded by another who came to the
conclusion that 'Mr. Bourinot lived in a mental fog, in
which no object was distinctly visible; and that while he
seemed to be under an overmastering impulse to speak,
he did not know what he wanted to say.'[8] Such outbursts
may have been motivated by disappointment; the opposition to exclusivity, self-perpetuation, and public funding
was more serious and the society would respond to these
issues in time.

The society was organized into four sections, with 20 fellows in each – I, 'Littérature Français, Histoire, Archéologie';
II, 'English Literature, History, Archaeology'; III, 'Math-
ematical, Physical and Chemical Sciences'; and IV, 'Geological and Biological Sciences.' According to Dawson's
recollections he would have preferred a purely scientific
society modelled on the Royal Society of London, and he
and some of Lorne's other guides had little difficulty in
naming creditable candidates for the scientific sections.
Daniel Wilson questioned the addition of the literary sections on the general grounds that while the humblest naturalist 'may contribute some new fact or observation in

science that will have its value' it was quite unclear what section II in particular was to do. 'Shall we write school-boy essays, or criticisms on the literature of the day; or theses on the want of literature?' Nor did he see the point of separating along language lines people who would presumably study the same history, any more than why there should be two language sections to investigate geology. Lorne, however, wanted to include French Canadians. Since they had paid less attention to science than to literature and history they seemed satisfied with a separate language section and left the science sections to English-Canadians.[9]

The objectives of the society, set out in its Act of Incorporation of 25 May 1883, were to encourage studies and investigations in literature and science; to publish transactions containing a record of proceedings, original papers, and documents; to offer prizes or other inducements for papers on 'subjects relating to Canada' and to aid research already begun that showed promise of ultimate value; and to assist in the collection of specimens for 'a Canadian Museum of archives, ethnology, archaeology and natural history.' Beyond this formal mandate were additional expectations made explicit at the first meeting of the society in 1882 by Lorne and Dawson, who became first president. Lorne emphasized the role of section I in maintaining the purity of the French language, and Dawson hoped that the Society's *Transactions* would become a vehicle for the best work in Canadian science.

Dawson knew that Canadian scientists scattered their publications in the journals of the local natural history societies and in the periodicals of such institutions as the Royal Society of London and the Boston Society of Natural History. He hoped that the *Transactions* would become instead the focus of their efforts and that the society, as a 'judicial body,' would act as an authority defining standards in the scientific fields. The dominion government granted the society $5,000 a year to pay for publishing the

Transactions, and Dawson anticipated that the organization would attract 'private benefactions' so that it could support research as well. Dawson proposed in addition that the *Transactions* be open to non-members and that the society affiliate with the local societies, which were already linked to it through its charter members. This was Dawson's response to those who charged that the new body was a closed elite. And finally he hoped – as did others then and since – that the society would constitute a pool of talent and detached experts who would be called on by governments for advice.[10]

The charter members of the society were to have greater influence in shaping its character than all such expectations. They represented a very wide assortment of talent, education, and profession: indeed the most striking feature of the 80 originals was the sheer diversity of their backgrounds and intellectual interests. There are, however, three general features of the first generation that stand out. The first is that a substantial number – about one-quarter in 1890 – were employed by governments as clerks in legislative assemblies or the House of Commons, as translators, in libraries (including the Library of Parliament), or in such government agencies as the Public Archives and the Geological Survey. In some cases what they did as civil servants had no bearing on their intellectual preoccupations. Both George Matthew, a Saint John geologist, and James LeMoine, who wrote of popular ornithology and historical legends of Quebec, earned their livings as customs collectors. The poet Archibald Lampman and the critic William LeSueur worked in the administration of the Post Office.

The second feature of the members was the significant proportion of clergymen. In 1882 there were five clerics in section I, four in section II. By 1908, four of the 26 fellows in section I were clergymen, as were nine of the 30 in II. This latter figure does not include such people as the historian George Wrong, the poet and civil servant Wilfred Campbell, or the literary journalist John Reade, all of whom were ordained Anglican priests who had abandoned their clerical careers. This career shift was, for theirs and the subsequent generation, by no means uncommon. Charles Hill-Tout, a British Columbia anthropologist, gave up theology for science; so too did Henry Marshall Tory, a major figure in the society in the years between the two world wars. Tory had a bachelor of divinity degree and had preached in Montreal for two years before returning permanently to mathematics and physics. Robert Falconer, who presided over the University of Toronto's transformation into a major scientific centre, was an ordained Presbyterian minister. The prominence of these clerics confirms the traditional idea of the clergy's important contribution to Canada's intellectual life. It suggests something more. Lorne Pierce, himself a clergyman turned publisher and literary promoter, caught something of the intellectual flavour of these backgrounds when, in characterizing a group of poets of the same generation, he wrote of 'the moral urgency of rectory and parsonage,' 'the general Victorian reticence,' and 'the standardized etiquette of college classroom, parish and government bureau.'[11]

An equally familiar occupation, at least in the two literary sections, was journalism. The career of George Stewart illustrates the many undertakings of those who made a living by their pens. He started out as a druggist, founded a stamp collectors' journal, ran *Stewart's Literary Quarterly Magazine* between 1867 and 1872, was chief editor of *Rose-Belford's Canadian Monthly*, and from 1879 to 1896 edited the Quebec (City) *Daily Chronicle*, to which he contributed literary appreciations of Carlyle, Longfellow, and Thoreau. Involvement in journalism – and its handmaiden, politics – was most pronounced among French-Canadian fellows, a surprising number of whom had held public office or had run in elections. Joseph Tassé, who guided the bill to incorporate the society through the House of Commons, had, like many in section I, undertaken classical studies and legal training and worked as a journalist, with *La Minerve*. In the 1870s he was a translator to the House of Commons; from 1878 to 1887 he represented Ottawa in Parliament. Joseph Edward Roy, best remembered for his *Bulletin des recherches historiques*, which he founded with his brother Pierre-Georges, was a notary, mayor of Lévis, and editor (1879–86) of *Le Quotidien*. There were, in contrast, comparatively few figures in section II who had run for – or held – public office: one of them, George Ross, had spoken in support of the incorporation bill in the Commons and was to become Ontario's minister of education.

Section I was distinctive in other ways. In contrast to the other sections in 1882 – in which 32 of 60 fellows had been born and educated in Britain (in section II only four were of Canadian birth) – all but one were born in Canada.[12] Section I was defined not only in terms of subjects and language; it was also the French-Canadian ethnic depart-ment. It found places for the representatives of the francophone minority outside Quebec. Senator Pascal Porrier was for many years an envoy of the Acadians; Judge L.A. Prud'homme of St Boniface, Manitoba, wrote many essays on Métis history and genealogy and saw these people as an integral part of the French-Canadian family who deserved to have their language rights respected. Members of sec-tion I also looked outward to France, where not a few had worked and travelled, and they treasured recognition from that nation through either prizes of the Institut français or membership in the Légion d'honneur.

Of the 80 charter members in 1882 only a quarter were attached to colleges; academics were only slightly more numerous in the two scientific departments, in which they constituted a third of the membership. The university teachers who had received academic appointments in the middle decades of the century were generalists who taught an astonishing spectrum of subjects and, as in Dawson's case, wandered the entire domain of natural history and geology. Loring Bailey of Fredericton published on the economic minerals of New Brunswick and prehistoric remains of humans as well as on his specialty – diatoms. Academics were outnumbered by civil servants, clergymen, and journalists – often journalist-politicians – and their variegated backgrounds and intellectual concerns imparted to the early society a heterogeneous character.

In its first three decades the Royal Society of Canada established its routines and conventions, meeting for three days in the third week of May – as near as possible to the queen's birthday or on the anniversary of the date on which Lorne arranged the first gathering – in Ottawa, usually at the Normal School or in the Carnegie Library (Principal McCabe of the former was made a member mainly because of his role as host). Apart from holding general business sessions and hearing the presidential address, the four sections convened separately and operated with considerable autonomy. Each had its own president, vice-president, and other officials.

Each section was responsible for electing new members, and this task turned out to be a major preoccupation: between 1882 and 1898 some 25 fellows died, and 11 either left Canada or had withdrawn from active participation. Initially nominations were made in writing by three fellows of a section in which a vacancy had occurred, and then the section voted from a printed list. A successful candidate had to secure two-thirds of the votes of the section. Should no one receive this degree of support the council of the society could select the candidate with the largest number of votes.[13] After 1904 candidates had to receive only the majority of votes in the relevant section.

It would be inordinately innocent to assume that nominations and elections were unaffected by friendships and other interests. The imperialist and writer on cavalry tactics Colonel G.T. Denison campaigned vigorously on behalf of his friend the poet Charles Mair, and Rev. George Patterson, the historian of Pictou county, sought the assistance of Dawson, another Pictonian, in order to become a member. In 1911 the professor of pathology at the University of Toronto solicited support from several fellows for two candidates from his university.[14] In 1899 Bourinot drew 'attention to what seems an absence of good taste on the part of some persons who wish from time to time to become connected with this society, and that is in pressing their personal claims with great pertinacity on the members of the section to which they have aspirations.'[15] Bourinot trusted that mere mention of such egregious behaviour would put a stop to it.

Fellowship in the Royal Society was seen as more than recognition of the intellectual achievement of an individual. In the late 1880s – only a few years after Nova Scotia elected a government pledged to repeal the union with Canada – George Lawson of Halifax urged that in electing members the society should aim at 'fair representation and encouragement to every province and every part of the Dominion' as the 'surest guarantee against the tendency to centralization which seemed to some of us from the first to menace it.' In 1893 council – which included the president of the sections, the president of the society, and such officials as editor and treasurer – also supported making membership as 'representative' as possible: 'Those universities and institutions which are already well represented in the sections, should even be ready to lay aside the claims of well qualified persons connected with themselves, so that the distant parts of the Dominion like British Columbia, Manitoba and Prince Edward Island may be recognized in the membership of the Royal Society.'[16] To a degree this advice was followed. Two decades later the distribution of fellows in section II indicated a compromise of sorts between centralization and representativeness: Ottawa had nine fellows, Toronto six, Montreal four, Quebec two, and Calgary, Halifax,

Kingston, Saint John, St John's, Westmount, and Winnipeg one each.

Lawson's remark about centralization carried another implication. Between 1882 and 1901 only two meetings of the society took place outside Ottawa; indeed in its first half-century only eight annual meetings occurred outside the capital. Bourinot was secretary from 1882 to 1902, edited the *Transactions*, and attended to most business matters between sessions. The office of the clerk of the Commons became in effect the clearing-house and administrative centre of the organization. After Bourinot's death these tasks were performed by other Ottawa-based secretaries – the scholarly queen's printer Samuel E. Dawson and the poet and deputy superintendent of Indian affairs Duncan Campbell Scott. In the first two decades of this century a local council of the society met in Scott's office and provided continuity. 'The R.S.C.,' grumbled one Montrealer and subsequent member, William Lighthall, 'has fallen into disfavour, even contempt, through burying itself [in Ottawa].'[17] While at the beginning it was anticipated that the society would meet in different centres, and there was nothing in the constitution preventing this, there were good reasons why it became so closely identified with the capital. 'It is necessary to remember,' wrote Bourinot, in rejecting a proposal for a meeting in Toronto, 'that nine-tenths of the members live between Ottawa, Kingston and Quebec and it is consequently possible to have a fair attendance at a relatively small cost in Ottawa, where there are twenty-five resident Fellows.'[18]

Another feature of the society that appeared early and became permanent was very unequal interest in its affairs displayed by the fellows. At annual meetings between 1882 and 1896 about half the members attended – a record that optimists compared favourably to participation in the (U.S) National Academy of Sciences or the American Historical Association. In 1894 Bourinot judged attendance over the previous four years 'exceedingly inadequate'[19] and explained this in terms of costs of travel, prior commitments of members, and, in some cases, advanced ages. Distance was certainly a factor: Rev. George Taylor of Nanaimo, BC, a student of marine fauna, elected in 1894, attended his first meeting in 1906! The society subsidized the travel expenses of those living east of Quebec and west of Toronto, but in 1912 the funds disbursed for this purpose were only $127.09. Disappointing attendance figures indicated that for some the society did not address any intellectual need. Goldwin Smith never attended, and John Watson, the idealist philosopher from Queen's, Richard Maurice Bucke, the alienist from the London Asylum, and Colonel Denison found little of interest in the society's deliberations, judging by their absenteeism. The society early adopted a working rule that those not attending for three years in succession without presenting a paper or giving satisfactory reasons for absences should be considered to have resigned. Though in the 1880s several individuals resigned or were placed on the 'retired list,' many of the apathetic remained. In 1906 sections were allowed to suspend the working rule until the next annual meeting, but this simply encouraged procrastination. Section II could not bring itself to consider the eviction of Colonel Denison, who in 1913 was its last living charter member. To have dealt resolutely with delinquents would have in fact diminished the society's claims to include intellectuals of renown and eroded its own prestige.

Thus there are two histories of the Royal Society. The first consisted of an ever-expanding list of names (the numbers in sections were increased to 25 in 1891 and 30 in 1899); the second is the story of a minority who earnestly tried to make the organization, in Bourinot's words, a 'working body, and not a purely honorary institution.'[20] The latter purpose involved not only paying attention to business affairs but also contributing to its meetings and the *Transactions*. In the early period William Dawson provided a paper, usually in fossil botany, every year, and George Matthew published a long series of reports on the fossil fauna of the Saint John group. In so far as publishing in the *Transactions* indicated commitment to the society, the most devoted in section II in the first generation were Bourinot, Patterson, Wilson, the Manitoba historian Rev. George Bryce, Samuel E. Dawson, the military historian Ernest Cruikshank, and corresponding member William F. Ganong. Some published one or two presentation pieces; others, like the best-selling novelist Rev. Charles W. Gordon, known better as Ralph Connor, and the journalist John Willison, offered nothing at all.

From the outset the society was handicapped by lack of sufficient funding to promote its larger purposes. Most of the government grant of $5,000 a year (increased in 1913 to $8,000) went to paying to publish the *Transactions*, and the only other revenue came from memberships at $2 a year (the price of a book), which was raised to five dollars in 1910. Most of this latter income was used to subsidize railway fares. In 1895 a committee examined the prospects of offering scholarships and research support and concluded that the best hope lay in private benevolence. It was a forlorn expectation. In 1898 the society had some $200 to aid scientific studies; in 1909 the president approached Lord Strathcona, whose munificence had supported many causes, with no result. Curiously, however, in 1910 the society had to its credit a sum of $5,000 received as an insurance claim on copies of its *Transactions* that had been destroyed by fire some time earlier. The society decided to invest this windfall in mortgages on western real estate and did not consider spending it on research.[21] The offering of prizes and medals and the supporting of research, much less assisting in collecting specimens, were clearly beyond the body's early resources.

The 'main work of the Society' and the most visible result of the efforts of members were its stout volumes of

Proceedings and Transactions. The government grant obligated the society to publish its proceedings and papers in order to make Canada's resources and possibilities better known abroad, and it was to give copies to the members of the House of Commons and Senate, judges, and lieutenant-governors. These volumes were the centre-piece of the society, and they grew relentlessly in size, each year the secretary reporting an increase in the number of pages – from 650 in 1887, for example, to 1,228 in 1907. Though the *Transactions* originally appeared in quarto form, a new series was begun in 1895 in octavo size, much to the benefit of readers, 'who found it almost impossible to use the present cumbrous volumes for purposes of study with any degree of comfort.'

Volumes were exchanged with domestic and foreign institutions: in 1909, 104 were distributed within Canada, in addition to those sent to members, politicians, and officials; 210 went to the United States, 103 to continental Europe, 86 to Britain, 29 to British colonies, and 10 to Central and South America. Samuel Dawson, who was in charge of this exchange network, wrote with some feeling: 'Above all things the most vexatious is to have a parcel for South America sent to Australia and one for New Zealand to Russia.' The society's volumes were looked on as emissaries of Canada to the international community and evidence, in G.M. Grant's phrase, that Canada was 'not wholly a barbarous country.'[22]

These exchanges with foreign institutions had one unintended effect. The accumulation of periodicals, bulletins, and reports – some 52 boxes by 1903 – underlined the society's need for a headquarters with library space. Only in 1913 was the society given a room in Ottawa's newly finished Victoria Memorial Museum (or National Museum) for the accumulations of some thirty years.

The record of its proceedings indicated an emergent corporate sense within the society and aspirations beyond

the narrowly scholarly. Again Bourinot was the crucial
figure: during his long editorship the records of proceedings grew ever more discursive and copious, carrying reports not merely of the society's business – elections, lobbying efforts – but summaries of the annual activities of
such government agencies as the tides and currents
surveys, Public Archives, experimental farms, and meterological service and reports of local societies affiliated with
the Royal Society. Bourinot aspired to make the proceedings 'as far as practicable, a complete summary of all scientific and literary work of Canadian societies,' a 'repetory
of all the intellectual work in this country.'²³

Though many bibliographies of current and past publications were printed in its volumes, the *Transactions* never
realized Bourinot's other hope – that it would review Canadian books with greater discernment than was customary in the newspapers. This aim of covering intellectual
life as comprehensively as possible was paralleled by increasing attention to current issues. After the mid-1890s
many subjects were brought to the attention of the society
by would-be reformers – the copyright question, the need
for a single text in Canadian history to be used throughout the country, the injurious effects of sensational journalism from 'New York and other places in the United
States,' 'the widespread use of defective English' and the
desirability of remedial action, and the necessity for free
public libraries. The engineer Sandford Fleming bubbled
over with improvements regarding international time-
keeping, the metric system, representation in the House
of Commons, and a telegraphic cable linking the components of the British Empire.

The conservation of natural resources was an abiding concern within the Royal Society from its first meeting in
1882, when it urged preservation of forests and promoted
tree planting by public or private means. William Saunders
underlined the economic self-interest implicit in efficient

use of forests. Both John Macoun and Robert Bell, as employees of the Geological Survey, travelled extensively in
the thinly settled parts of Canada, and both were struck
by the contrast between what they actually saw and the
popular perception of unlimited natural resources. Bell
reported that the northern forest was one-third newly
burnt, a third second growth of all ages, and only the
remainder full-grown trees. 'We have been told,' added
Macoun in 1894, 'that we have immense forests of white
pine still untouched and that generations will pass before
we can destroy it all. The same was said of the buffalo.'
He saw little hope for changing attitudes and behaviour,
'for viciousness, carelessness, cupidity and supineness of
governments and people ... will continue.' Section IV in
1895 protested the needless waste of forests by fire and
advocated the removal of large tracts from lumbering in
order to protect water supplies. Charles Mair spoke from
experience when he contrasted the large numbers of bison in the west in the 1860s and their virtual extermina-
tion within two decades. 'There is perhaps no fact in the
natural history of America which brings such reproach on
civilized man as the reckless and almost total destruction
of the bison.' And the representative of Newfoundland in
the society, Rev. Moses Harvey, pointed to signs of decline in that colony's cod fishery and urged a program of
restocking inshore waters and stations to study marine
biology as a national responsibility.[24]

Though the society took up Harvey's suggestion in 1892
it was only in 1897 that a committee of the British Association for the Advancement of Science struck a lobby
that convinced Canada's Department of Marine and Fisheries to support, on a trial basis for five years, investigation of food supplies and conditions of fish life in general.
One of the first topics explored was the effect of water
pollution. By 1907 there were four marine biological
stations – at Departure Bay near Nanaimo, BC, Seven
Islands in the Gulf of St Lawrence, St Andrews, New

Brunswick, and Georgian Bay.[25] A similar strategy was pursued in regard to observations of tides and currents. It was the British Association's Montreal meeting in 1884 that drew the matter to the attention of the society, which thereafter repeatedly memorialized the government with the backing of shipping interests and the Montreal Board of Trade. The Department of Marine and Fisheries began to study hidden currents and tides in a small way, but only in 1905 did a parliamentary appropriation commit the state to maintain such a survey.

In these two matters of tidal currents and the fisheries the suggestions of the society were invariably made along with support from other groups, and the role of the British Association was especially important. When after 1900 the issue of the conservation of resources became more pressing the dominion did not turn to the Royal Society but created its own advisory body, the Commission of Conservation, in 1909. An institution that convened three days a year was an ineffectual source of advice to governments, even though fellows of the society were notable figures in these ventures.

This was the fate also of a number of other memorials from the society, ranging from persistent support for a national museum to house the collections of the Geological Survey to backing for a national library. Those familiar with the lobbying activities of the society before 1914 seldom claimed that it exerted influence on politicians. That impression was created in the 1920s with assertions that the society had been instrumental 'in bringing about the establishment of such institutions as the Victoria Museum, the Meterological Service, the Public Archives, the National Gallery.' Such contentions were frequently advanced in welcoming governors general as patrons of the society or in adding force to requests for additional funding. Yet the origins of the Public Archives and the Meterological Service antedate the founding of the Royal Society, and in the case of the National Museum the

efforts of the Geological Survey were probably more decisive. One careful historian of the society's lobbying efforts before 1900 concluded that there was no instance in
which the society, operating on its own, succeeded in any
of its objectives.[26] In one case it was simply unlucky. In
1904 the society asked for financial support for a meeting
in Canada of the International Geological Congress; it was
promised that if it undertook the invitations and management for the visit the government would put $25,000 at its
disposal. Robert Bell made his way with the invitation to
Vienna, where the congress was in session, only to learn
that the Mexican government had acted more swiftly and
had been chosen as the site of the next congress.[27]

The early fellows attempted to offset the reproof that they
had created a closed coterie by forging links beyond the
society. Their meetings and the *Transactions* were open to
papers written by non-members; in 1894 of some 30 papers presented to section IV 10 were given by people outside the society. This remained a common practice in all
sections, a fact that gave Bourinot considerable satisfaction, as denying the 'exclusive character which some persons would attribute to its organization.'[28] This custom
became part of the strategy for recruiting new fellows; the
reading of papers written by promising candidates was
frequently followed by their nomination and election.
Membership was confined to residents of Canada and
Newfoundland, but very early the society created a category of 'corresponding member.' Among the first was
the American historian Francis Parkman. Corresponding
membership in some cases was far from merely honorary.
William F. Ganong, who was born in New Brunswick but
taught at Smith College in Northampton, Massachusetts,
was a prolific contributor to the society's publications for
over fifty years.

    The society was also affiliated to pre-existing local natu-
ral history and scientific societies and to local historical

societies, which appeared in increasing numbers in the late nineteenth century. The original members had very close ties with local scientific bodies – Dawson with the Natural History Society of Montreal, Loring Bailey with the Natural History Society of New Brunswick, George Lawson with the Nova Scotia Institute of Natural Science, and Wilson with the Royal Canadian Institute in Toronto. In 1900 there were some 36 affiliated societies (13 scientific) whose delegates were invited to present reports of activities to the annual meeting of the Royal Society, and this many of them did in lavish detail, covering not merely their publications and lecture programs but also the state of their museums and libraries, categories of books borrowed, and exchange programs. (The Royal Canadian Institute in 1894 received exchanges from some 540 societies – approximately the same number as the Royal Society itself).[29]

These local associations varied considerably in nature. One of the most successful, the Ottawa Field Naturalists' Club, had over three hundred members after the turn of the century, including 25 fellows of the Royal Society; others, such as the Miramichi Natural History Society, represented the enthusiasm of only a few. Some – the Ottawa Literary and Scientific Society and the Manitoba Historical and Scientific Society, for example – sponsored what were in effect municipal libraries and reading rooms.

These organizations were partly social and partly scientific, and most were devoted to popularizing science, especially natural science. After the turn of the century they promoted nature study in the schools, and the Natural History Society of Montreal turned to reform. It cooperated with the local of the National Council of Women, the Tuberculosis League, the Pure Milk League, and hospitals in giving lectures to artisans on direct application of science to daily occupations, sanitation, and infectious diseases.[30]

Nature study remained a major concern with some members of the Royal Society. The Botanical Club of

Canada was set up in 1891, mainly at Lawson's initiative, to encourage local collectors, field clubs, and recording of seasonal events in natural history and meteorology. This latter activity was vigorously pursued by Alexander MacKay, superintendent of education for Nova Scotia, who inspired teachers and school children to record the dates of the fruiting of plants, autumn frosts, pipping of frogs, and appearances of birds. These 'phenological observations' were collated and published in the Royal Society's *Transactions*.

The society also imitated the practice of the local bodies by offering a public lecture in conjunction with its annual meeting. The first, in 1892, was given by the McGill physiologist T. Wesley Mills on science in the schools. Members were not always gratified by the response: in 1914 a physicist lamented that during the Montreal meeting some eleven thousand people attended a wrestling match while few availed themselves of an invitation to meetings and discussions with the Royal Society.[31]

The relationship between the Royal Society and the affiliated groups was taken by some to suggest a 'federation ... of societies recognizing the Royal Society as a centre.' That was some distance from an early remark that the society itself was 'the foster-daughter of the Canadian scientific societies.'[32] In any case these delegates' reports to the annual meetings were not universally appreciated. One representative of the Ottawa Literary and Scientific Society in the mid-1890s commented in his diary that such reports were greeted with indifference and polite applause 'for what is not very evident – whether for the substance or for the fact that the end has been reached.' A few, he added, were in French 'and hence almost Greek.'[33]

These contacts were disrupted by the Great War; they were also victims of changes in the Royal Society itself. When local reporting resumed in the late 1920s only three of 45 affiliates submitted reports to confirm their existence, and formal ties with local organizations were termi-

nated in 1940. By then it was not uncommon for professional and highly specialized scientists to 'regret the passing of the amateur worker in the field of local geology – a
field which owed so much in the past to men of self-
trained but observant mind.'[34]

Like the local groups the Royal Society of Canada perpetuated a tradition of distancing itself from contentious
religious and political issues. Indeed Bourinot believed
that the society, by encouraging the coming together of
people widely differing in politics, religion, and opinion,
was helping to break down asperities and prejudices. Sara
Jeannette Duncan was not far off the mark when in 1886
she characterized the 'journalistic pabulum' consumed by
most people in Ontario as 'politics and vituperation, tem-
perance and vituperation, religion and vituperation.'[35]
While some in the society envisaged the body as standing
above such fanaticism, encouraging circumspection and
decorum, this did not mean that the organization and its
members were unaffected by the conditions of their time.
Contemporary developments obtruded into the erudite
pages of the *Transactions*, often in disconcerting ways, as
when two fellows of section I in the 1890s discoursed on
the menace of socialism and the proper place of women
in society.

Far more obvious, however, was the support for imperial unity among Anglo Canadians in the society. The
Imperial Federation League was founded in London,
England, in 1884, and its offshoots soon appeared in
Canada. Imperial unity became a rallying cry for those
who advocated closer ties to Britain as a counterweight to
the threat of annexation to the United States, and it appealed
to the same groups that were so strongly represented in
the Royal Society – educators, writers, and moral leaders,
such as G.M. Grant. Imperialists were well established in
section II; Colonel G.T. Denison, in his only presentation
to the society, treated imperial unity as an inheritance

from the United Empire Loyalists, and Bourinot's numerous essays on Canadian development traced ever-expanding political liberty from introduction of responsible government, through Confederation, to what he hoped would be an imperial union that would strengthen the empire and give Canadians a higher position in its councils. Equally fervent were William Kirby, Bishop O'Brien of Halifax, George Parkin, and Wilfred Campbell, whose *Sagas of Vaster Britain* (1914) made him an unofficial laureate of empire. The British Association for the Advancement of Science met in Canada in 1884, 1897, 1909, and 1924 and seemed a visible testament of imperial cooperation, despite the growing links – also expressed by the Royal Society – with scientists in the United States. In 1887, which was celebrated as the fiftieth anniversary of Queen Victoria's accession, and 'when plans for imperial federation are before the public,' William Dawson proposed an imperial geological union.[36] Sandford Fleming championed the Pacific cable linking Canada to Fiji, New Zealand, and Australia as a nervous system for the empire. As well, some English scientists recruited by Canadian universities became members of the society in the period before 1914; the botanist A.H.R. Buller of the University of Manitoba is reputed to have crossed the Atlantic 65 times. Such British institutions as the Cavendish Laboratories at Cambridge were magnets for the Canadian born, such as John C. McLennan of Toronto.

These affinities with empire were conveyed by the seal of the society, adopted in 1899: the royal arms, encircled by the arms of the Canadian provinces. 'The Imperial idea,' ran the description, 'is also conveyed by the fact that the points [of the arms] of the seven provinces converge towards the motherland represented by the Royal Arms.'[37] In his presidential address in 1900 Rev. William Clark of Trinity College, Toronto, concluded with a subject on many minds – the war in South Africa, in which over 7,000 Canadian volunteers would serve. If the Royal Society had any general end in view it must be the advancement of human civilization, and, if ever there was a war undertaken with this end, it was the struggle against the Boers. 'The imperial idea,' he said, 'which floated before us as an unembodied principle, has now entered into our heart and soul.'[38] In 1914 – the year the Marquess of Lorne died – this would be true again.

2

History and Ethnology

The founding of the Royal Society of Canada coincided with increasing interest in the Canadian past, which was expressed in the ever-growing numbers of publications, the appearance of many local historical societies, and such romantic historical novels as William Kirby's *The Golden Dog* (1877), set in the last days of New France, and Jean Talon Lesperance's *The Bastonnais* (1877), a tale of the American invasion of 1775–6.[1] It was apparent also in the determination to search out, preserve, and reprint authentic historical documents, to mark historical sites, and to celebrate the memories they evoked. The Royal Society and the affiliated historical societies became major outlets for this enthusiasm for recovering the past, and the literary departments of its *Transactions* in both French and English were dominated by historical studies.

This fascination with the past was nourished by a delight in remote and picturesque customs and antiquities that owed much to the example of Sir Walter Scott's borderland tales and the series of volumes by the American historian Francis Parkman on the struggle between Britain and France for mastery of North America, which were widely admired, at least in English Canada, for vivid narrative and evocation of scenes and were thought to have elevated writing about Canada to a new level. The possibilities for historical writing were being advanced by accumulation of documents by the Public Archives since 1872 and by the publication of sources by the Quebec government. This activity was reinforced by the local historical societies, which after 1880 were especially numerous in the older districts of Ontario, in Montreal, and, to a lesser degree, in Nova Scotia and New Brunswick. Of the 36 organizations affiliated with the Royal Society by 1900 some two-thirds were historical in character; at that time the Ontario Historical Society – with an estimated membership of 1,200 – encompassed 20 affiliates of its own, including a group from the Six Nations of the Grand River and two women's societies in Toronto and Ottawa.[2]

The type of history propagated within these bodies and by those who were members of the Royal Society was highly particularistic and documentary, and, as in the practice of natural history, it seemed that every fact was of inestimable value and worthy of notice. Thus a characteristic feature of historical reportage was listing – original settlers in an area, members of the House of Assembly of Upper Canada, or those who served in the Queen's Rangers in the Revolutionary War. No less intriguing was the challenge of establishing exactly the routes and landfalls of Cabot, Cartier, and other explorers, the location of fur trade posts, and the disposition of troops on the Plains of Abraham, or describing such relics as the Basque tombstone at Placentia, Newfoundland, the coinage of Nova Scotia, or the Canadian snowshoe. James LeMoine devoted an entire article to proving that Richard Montgomery's assault on the town of Quebec occurred on 1 January 1776, not 31 December 1775 as had been thought; and Rev. George Bryce of Winnipeg, after dipping into the archives of the Hudson's Bay Company as well as the holdings of the British Museum, was able to add a previously unknown 26 years to the career of Pierre Esprit Radisson.

Not a few of the historians in the Royal Society made the collection and publication of documents their life's work. Archdeacon William O. Raymond, rector of St Mary's

Church in Saint John, wrote extensively on local history in newspapers, supported the New Brunswick Historical Society, and compiled and published the papers of Edward Winslow, an administrator in the early days of the colony; and Ernest A. Cruikshank, an austere and matter-of-fact military officer, who reported to the Royal Society on the activities of the many historical societies in the Niagara Peninsula, issued nine volumes of documents on the military engagements on the Niagara frontier in the War of 1812, five volumes of John Graves Simcoe's correspondence, and three more containing letters of the administrator Peter Russell. The Royal Society itself took up the cause of printing historical sources: in 1907, 252 of the 364 pages contributed to the *Transactions* by section II were devoted to the Talbot Papers and the journal of Anthony Henday. In 1884 George Bryce had appealed for a group devoted to the issuing of sources and reprints of rare books; for a time the Royal Society, partially performed this function, but only the Champlain Society, founded in 1905, truly fulfilled that goal.

The mode of historical investigation represented in the society persisted well into the 1930s, though it was by then considered in some quarters to be increasingly anachronistic and antiquarian. Two of the most industrious chroniclers in the inter-war decades were judges elected fellows in 1917 – Frederic W. Howay of the County Court of New Westminster, BC, and W.R. Riddell, a justice of the Ontario Supreme Court. Howay's main effort was a series of five reports listing the trading vessels in the maritime fur trade on the Pacific coast between 1785 and 1825; Riddell (who in his lifetime wrote 1,258 articles, mostly relentless citations of legislation and judicial decisions)[3] showered section II with ten communications in 1928 (three were published) and eight the next year. The legal training and practice of these two men profoundly affected their sense of history – they paid very close attention to the written record and prized sobriety of statement, methodical attention to detail, factual accuracy, and impartiality. Their judicial approach and factualism were shared by such of their peers as James H. Coyne, registrar of deeds of Elgin county, Ontario, and both Rev. E.H. Oliver from Saskatoon, who published a list of 1,588 names of the heads of families who lived in the District of Saskatchewan in 1888, and Arthur S. Morton, a Presbyterian minister before he became a professor of history at the University of Saskatchewan, who excelled in establishing the precise locations of trading posts in the west.

This type of history was by and large written by members of the society for whom history was an avocation, who had close ties with provincial and local historical societies, and who saw their mission as cultivation of popular interest in the past. For all their arid factualism, they represented, as did the older naturalists, a world of learning that was accessible, even at the edges populist, as is suggested by the case of Frank G. Roe, who was by turns homesteader, locomotive engineer, and self-taught scholar, whose papers on the plains bison and Indian hunting practices found a welcome place in the *Transactions* of the Royal Society.

Preservation of documents and accurate establishment of facts were connected to the safeguarding of historic sites and buildings and commemorating significant events. Such activity was a major preoccupation of the local historical societies in the three decades after 1880, especially in the Niagara district, where attention focused on the battlefields of the War of 1812, caring for burial grounds, and exerting pressure on governments to erect memorials. The Numismatic and Antiquarian Society of Montreal was equally active in marking historic places with tablets, and in 1891 the Royal Society supported its successful efforts to preserve Château Ramezay, built in the early eighteenth century and residence of British governors, from the prevalent 'spirit of vandalism.' In the east Senator Pascal Porrier reported on the delapidation of sites in the Maritimes, especially Louisbourg. In Winnipeg, George Bryce regreted 'the act of vandalism' that demolished Fort Garry except for the front gateway and, as a leader in the Manitoba Historical and Scientific Society, encouraged the raising of a monument commemorating the skirmish at Seven Oaks in 1816. There were limits to what was considered acceptable in memorializing history: the Royal Society in 1901 reprimanded those who wanted to put up a marker to Richard Montgomery in Quebec, a proposal that excited considerable public outcry.

The society actively promoted commemoration of the 400th anniversary of the voyages in 1497 and 1498 of the Cabots, which coincided with Queen Victoria's diamond jubilee in 1897. The exact site of their landfall was hotly debated by several historians in the *Transactions*; the society as such prudently refrained from endorsing either Cape Breton or Newfoundland. On the meaning of the celebration, however, there was no doubt: the society held a meeting in Halifax for the occasion and presented a brass tablet (at a cost of $1,000), which was mounted at the entrance of Province House and unveiled by the governor general. The inscription observed that the Cabots' voyage 'gave to England a claim upon the continent which the colonizing spirit of her sons made good in later times,' and it noted that the tablet was placed on the sixtieth anniversary of the accession to the throne of Victoria, 'during whose beneficent reign the Dominion of Canada has extended from the shores, first seen by Cabot and English sailors four hundred years before, to the far Pacific coast.' Some saw this celebration of the Cabots as a response to the extreme glorification of Columbus at the Chicago World's Fair in 1893.[4]

After the turn of the century the Royal Society threw its support behind the movement to preserve places of historic and scenic interest, and thanks to its efforts and those of the local societies the Historical Landmarks Associa-

tion was established in 1907. In 1919 the latter was succeeded by the Historic Sites and Monuments Board of
Canada with the responsibility of advising the govern-
ment on places worthy of commemoration. In 1922 the
Historical Landmarks Commission was transformed into
the Canadian Historical Association. Its first meeting in
Ottawa took place at the same time as that of the Royal
Society, and relations in the early years were intimate.
The Canadian Historical Association drew heavily on the
local and provincial societies that the Royal Society had
encouraged and also on such stalwarts as Bryce, Coyne,
Cruikshank, and Howay. In fact, fewer than a seventh of
its members in 1923 were connected to universities or
archives. Together with the quarterly journal the *Canadian
Historical Review*, which in 1920 replaced the 24-year-old
Review of Historical Publications relating to Canada, the new
association initially appeared to supplement and expand
the work of the Royal Society. In time, however, this offspring supplanted and diminished the role of the society
in cultivating Canadian historical studies.[5]

It would oversimplify the case to leave the impression
that these 'amateur' historians were obsessed with the
preliminaries to history rather than with interpretation of
the past. There were a few who sometimes stood back
and reflected on the nature of written history, frequently
prompted by the claims of 'scientific history.' The most
extreme case for this view was made by a self-confident
holder of a fresh PhD from Leipzig – Hervey Bowman –
who argued at length that the historian must deal with
documents and solve problems with the 'same obedience
to fundamental scientific principles as is required by the
chemist, or the mathematician or the engineer.' The philosophical civil servant William D. LeSueur, who had turned
his hand to history with biographies of Count Frontenac
and William Lyon Mackenzie and who communicated
Bowman's papers to the society, was not so certain. He

told the Royal Society in 1913 that it was not impossible to get dates, names, and places right and to reproduce documents and treaties exactly. But what the historian made of such information was influenced by insights into human nature and the social environment of the times. Thus written history was subject to human limitations; the past can never be reconstructed with finality, much less totality. Still, LeSueur recognized that the practice of history had advanced considerably in the preceding half-century, especially in regard to impartiality and what he called 'a note of appeasement' – while history dealt with conflict it should not perpetuate past dissension but rather should aim at healing divisions and enlarging our appreciation of human fallibility. When LeSueur turned to the difficulty of revising history where interests and prejudices were at stake he must have spoken with some emotion: his biography of Mackenzie, who he found had a master passion for 'scolding, reviling, jeering,' had been kept from publication by the rebel's grandson, William Lyon Mackenzie King, who sat in the audience.[6]

Like their counterparts in section II the French Canadians were dedicated to the study of the past; even the poetry that their section regularly printed was often dedicated to memories, as was the case with Napoléon Legendre's 'La cloche,' which hinged on the turning points of 1759, 1775, 1812, and 1837. They tended to concentrate on the heroic age of colonization and missions, on genealogies and sketches of parishes, families, and dioceses, and on biographies of intendants, governors, and clergy. Their approach to the past was exemplified by the two-volume life of Bishop Laval written by abbé Auguste Honoré Gosselin, a seven-volume genealogical dictionary of families since 1608 by Mgr Cyprien Tanguay, and the bibliography by Narcisse Dionne, librarian of the Quebec legislature, of books, pamphlets, journals, and reviews published in Quebec between 1764 and 1904. E.Z. Massicotte, city of

Montreal archivist, was a regular contributor to the *Transactions* on such subjects as the census of that town in 1741 – a listing of 1,474 names, house by house, street by street.

The most active and productive historian in section I was Benjamin Sulte, who published 45 papers (five in English) in 40 years. Apart from his multi-volume history of the French Canadians, Sulte wrote some 3,000 articles, which appeared in 106 periodicals. These were too numerous, wrote his charitable obituarist, Aegidius Fauteux, to be of equal value; in fact many of them were research notes and excerpts from documents.[7] From 1882 to 1923 Sulte was an ever-present figure in the Royal Society, as organizer and translator, and there were times, as in 1896, when his efforts filled up most of the space allotted to section I. Sulte was a maverick among the French historians; he left school at ten and worked in a country store, as pursar on a steamer, bookkeeper, and cloth dealer, and thus he missed the customary education in classical college and seminary. An enthusiast for military ventures (and history) Sulte volunteered during the Fenian Raids and became a protégé of Cartier, who helped with his appointment as translator to the House of Commons in 1867 and the Militia Department in 1870. He was a rarity among the members of section I in that he actively supported imperial unity, translated 'God Save the King' into French, and when in Toronto to lecture to the Canadian Military Institute stayed with Denison, who shared his martial ardour. Self-taught and combative, Sulte represented a liberal strain in French-Canadian thought. Like Senator L.O. David, he opposed clerical intervention in politics, and in his historical essays he treated the missions to the Huron in the early seventeenth century as a wasted effort and questioned the idealization of the seigneurial system as ensuring social harmony and racial solidarity. Yet on other subjects he was orthodox, defending the untainted stock of the original immigrants to New France, insisting that they remained uncontaminated by Indian blood, and emphasizing the purity of their language.

Sulte was also exceptional in the society because he was one of a very few who crossed the sectional boundaries separating French from English. In 1897 he presented papers to both sections – one on Marie de l'Incarnation in French, and a report on the literature of Quebec, 1734–1830, in English. In the same year James LeMoine, a member of section I, spoke to section II on archival holdings in Canadian history. Like Sulte, LeMoine bridged the linguistic divide; a legend that he recorded inspired Kirby's *The Golden Dog*, and the two were lifelong friends. The novel was translated into French by another fellow, Pamphile Lemay. There were other personal contacts, usually outside the institutional confines of the Society; the Toronto historian George M. Wrong, for example, corresponded with abbé Henri-Raymond Casgrain. And between the world wars Marius Barbeau, who had studied at Oxford as a Rhodes scholar, taken his doctorate in science at the Sorbonne, and been appointed anthropologist at the National Museum in 1911, frequently offered papers to both language sections on the folkways of French Canada and western Aboriginal groups. In general, however, such initiatives were uncommon; they were infrequently reciprocated.

The first joint meeting of the two language sections took place in 1917, the fiftieth anniversary of Confederation and the year of the bitter division over conscription, and was arranged by Sulte, Wrong, and the economic historian Adam Shortt. This innovation seemed such a rewarding experience that the two sections resolved to make joint sessions regular features of annual meetings. This was done twice in the early 1920s but was not followed up in any systematic fashion.

A lasting feature of the relations of French and English historians within the society was the penchant of the French for periodically reproving members of section II for holding mistaken views. Abbé Casgrain caused quite a stir in 1888 when he not only censured the decision to deport the Acadians but also charged that important evidence favourable to their case had been suppressed.[8] In 1888 Hector Fabre, agent for the Canadian government in Paris and a charter member of the society, took aim at Francis Parkman, hero to many in section II who found his judgments agreeable. Parkman's treatment of the French and British imperial struggle as a conflict of torpor versus virility, the past against the future, he argued, confused simple force of numbers with defects in colonial and social policy. J.C. Dent's history of the Union period and the views of A.G. Doughty, dominion archivist, on the alignment of troops on the Plains of Abraham came in for equally forceful criticisms in section I, as did William Henry Drummond's habitant poems, for misrepresenting the speech of French Canadians. In a similar vein Jean-Léon Olivier Maurault, rector of the Université de Montréal, chastised Lorne Pierce's *Outline History of Canadian Literature* (1927) for beginning with the British Conquest and undervaluing the writings of French explorers and missionaries as contributors to literature.[9] Such corrections were usually published in section I's part of the *Transactions* and were addressed to its members.

The relative isolation of the two language groups was reinforced by those English-language historical writers who dealt with subjects of considerable interest to the French but offered their findings to section II. Sometimes these efforts were unexpectedly sympathetic. In 1908 William Wood, an authority on military and naval history, eulogized Marie de l'Incarnation on the occasion of proposals for her beatification and judged that she was as important a founder of Canada as any man. Rev. William Withrow, editor of the *Canadian Methodist Magazine*, exalted the Jesuit martyrs for their 'grandest traits of Christian manhood,' 'purity of character,' and 'nobility of soul.' These historians also took great satisfaction with what was later accepted as obvious: in his presidential address of 1908 – which coincided with the celebration of the Quebec tercentenary – Samuel Dawson drew attention to the 'unification of our history' and considered it remarkable that the English part of the population had come to see the French regime as part of its own history.[10] Sulte, too, thought it singular that the people of Ontario and the Maritimes should regard Champlain as one of the founders of the country. These were small victories, considering the isolation of the two historical traditions within the society.

The character of the Aboriginal peoples and their tribal divisions, languages, and customs figured prominently in the *Transactions* before the turn of the century. Though archaeology had been a long-standing interest in the natural history societies, which reported discoveries of prehistoric remains as well as ambitious speculations on human origins, the papers offered to the Royal Society concentrated on ethnology and anthropology whose boundaries seemed vague and uncertain. In 1887 six of the eight papers in section II were ethnological, including one by Franz Boas on Baffin Island Inuit mythology and customs. Christian missionaries had a continuing interest in the languages and customs of those they endeavoured to change, and Indian vocabularies were conspicuous in their intellectual efforts. The French-born Sulpician Jean-André Cuoq responded to denigrations of the languages of the North American Indians by defending the complexity and beauty of Algonquin grammar, on which he published an extensive study in 1892. George M. Dawson acquired a good deal of information about the Aboriginal groups of British Columbia, including comparative vocabularies, incidental to his geological reconnaissance.

For all his misgivings about section II, Daniel Wilson did his best to contribute his own papers in ethnology and encourage others as well. Though a professor of English and history at the University of Toronto before he became its president, Wilson was widely known for *Pre-historic Man* (1862), a plump, two-volume work that rejoiced in the sheer diversity of expression of the aesthetic and inventive faculties of humankind. For Wilson there existed – had always existed – a fundamental unity of humanity: different levels of technological development were due more to environment than to different degrees of potential. He was fascinated by the Aboriginal peoples of the New World, moreover, because he saw them as contemporary illustrations of what prehistoric peoples of Europe must have been like. The ethnological history of the Old World was repeating itself in the new. Wilson published in the *Transactions* on palaeolithic dexterity and trade and commerce in the stone age and urged that more attention be paid to the funeral rites of Aboriginal people, the nature of the 'half-breed' (the Métis made their last stand in 1885), and the dialect of the habitant.[11]

Some of the papers on Native peoples were sympathetic for their time, a period in which Canada's assimilationist Indian policy was codified and applied vigorously in the west. The historian of Pictou, Rev. George Patterson, explained the extinction of the Beothuk of Newfoundland – 'one of the darkest pictures on the pages of time' – as growing out of the encounter of a people who generously shared all their material goods and expected the same liberality of the Europeans with rude fishermen and hunters who misunderstood them and were unrestrained by law. The lieutenant-governor of Manitoba, John Christian Schultz, reported to the society on the Inuit (he used the name they gave themselves); he admired the ingenuity displayed in hunting implements and clothing, emphasized their fearlessness, and considered that they should be left alone until the time came to 'economize' them as hunters, boatmen, or guides.[12]

On a more sophisticated level Horatio Hale advanced the cause of comparative philology as the true basis of anthropology. American born and educated as a lawyer,

Hale lived at Clinton   near the Six Nations and was a
friend of Chief George Johnson, the father of Pauline Johnson. In 1883 he published *The Iroquois Book of Rites*, a study
of the condolence ceremony at which a deceased chief
was publicly lamented and his successor installed in office. Like Wilson, Hale rejected the notion that technological progress was the measure of human intelligence and
potential and insisted that language was the only certain
test of the affinities of races and of mental capacity in
general. Referring to an Indian language, Hale claimed
that it was 'one of the most remarkable emanations of the
human intellect' in its varied expressions, wealth of in-
flection, and complexity, and he argued that the 'philologist perceives in the speech of the savage the promise of
capacity for any duties of civilization.' Hale admired the
ceremonies, institutions, and character of the Iroquois
peoples, who had been treated by historians (he might
have been thinking of Parkman and Sulte) as fierce and
cruel savages. It was the circumstances of their contact
with Europeans that led to this view; Europeans arrived
with the intention of taking possession of the country and
displacing the Natives. 'The Indians were at once thrown
on the defensive. From the very beginning they fought
not merely for their land, but for their lives.' They should
be judged not merely by their qualities displayed in war
but by their social life in peace. They were, Hale found,
'among the most kindly and generous of men. Constant
good humour, unfailing courtesy, ready sympathy with
distress, and a truly lavish liberality, mark their inter-
course with one another.'[13]

   In 1884 Hale was made research director of the Committee on the North-Western Tribes set up at the Montreal
meeting of the British Association for the Advancement
of Science. Subsidized by the British Association, this committee included Wilson and G.M. Dawson, and it relied
on the cooperation of such missionaries as John Maclean
and 'amateur' anthropologists as Charles Hill-Tout of Brit-

ish Columbia. It eventually published eight volumes, but efforts to extend it into an ethnological survey that would include the study of French-Canadian folk culture as well as the new European immigrants foundered despite support from the Royal Society. The only result of another effort to bring into existence an ethnographic survey of Canada at the British Association's meeting in Winnipeg in 1909 was the creation of an Anthropology division within the Museum Branch of the Geological Survey in 1910. The appointment of Edward Sapir, one of Boas's students, to this position is usually taken as an indication of the displacement of an indigenous, amateur Canadian tradition by one oriented to Boas and the United States.[14] In any case, reports of Indian vocabularies and grammars and descriptions of Aboriginal peoples, which were so conspicuous in the *Transactions* in the 1880s and 1890s, declined drastically about this time, a signal, perhaps, of the general dwindling of interest in the 'Indian problem.' One of the last reports, curiously, was compiled by a group of chiefs of the Six Nations, who, encouraged by Duncan Campbell Scott, published an account of the origins of their Confederacy.[15]

In so far as ethnology was subsequently developed within the Royal Society it depended on scholars attached to the National Museum such as William J. Wintemberg, who focused on archaeological sites and placenames, and New Zealand–born Diamond Jenness, an authority on the Inuit, who seldom shared his wisdom with the society's members. Marius Barbeau, who had been a student with Jenness at Oxford and who became a member in 1916, was in contrast devoted, moving with ease from section I to section II and publishing abundantly in both languages. Since the 1880s there had been deepening interest in the legends of old Quebec, and after 1900 the curiosity of several French-Canadian members converged on folk culture. Sulte was involved in efforts to establish an ethnological survey that would cover such subjects, and Léon

Gérin, as is seen below, had already explored the sociology of habitant families. Barbeau extended this interest out of the conviction that French-Canadian oral traditions and domestic arts, and distinct regional forms of the French language, were being eroded by industrialization, the spread of public education, and out-migration. Thus his phonograph recordings of songs, legends, and anecdotes arose out of the same sort of determination that had lent a sense of urgency to those, such as Wilson, who had earlier pleaded for collection of Indian lore and relics before these peoples disappeared altogether. Always Barbeau was overwhelmed with variety and diversity, and he showed scant patience with those who emphasized the homogeneity of the French spoken throughout Quebec.[16] In time he extended his range and made records of some 8,500 texts and some 5,000 melodies of French, English, and Indian songs.

3

The Sciences

The Royal Society of Canada was unusual but not unique among learned societies in combining literature and history with the sciences. Its first 30 years bore out Daniel Wilson's judgment that the sciences were in a stronger position than literary studies in the actual development of the society and its relations with other institutions. Indeed, to observers at the turn of the century the fecundity of scientific publication worldwide was astounding: the Toronto librarian James Bain informed the Royal Canadian Institute that some 30,000 scientific periodicals were published each year and estimated that about 600,000 articles appeared annually – nearly 2,000 every day. From the beginning section IV – devoted to geology and biology – underlined the standing of the Geological Survey of Canada,[1] which was represented by six employees in 1882. Ten years later there were 11 geologists, seven botanists, and four zoologists; the section was kept from becoming a preserve of the survey only because some of its employees preferred 'not voting at all and letting the vacancies stand open until good men, not on our staff, turn up.'[2] The *Transactions* borrowed from the research of the Geological Survey; it became dependent also on the Experimental Farm in Ottawa for reports on soil chemistry and plant breeding; on the marine biological stations, which supported such studies as J. Playfair McMurrich's inquiry into the age and life cycle of sockeye salmon, as determined by concentric lines on their scales, and on the tides and currents survey.

Section IV perpetuated a mode of science that had been central to the natural history inventory – description and classification of newly discovered fossils and lists of plants, butterflies, and shells. Some members were omnivorous (or indiscriminate) in their intellectual tastes and not easily categorized into discrete scientific disciplines. Robert Bell collected Indian legends and published on such disparate topics as the Canadian porcupine, distribution of trees, character of ice, and the petroleum fields of southwestern Ontario. He exemplified the tradition of the scientist-explorer as did his colleague, John Macoun the botanist, who took as much delight in calculating the distances he travelled on his collecting expeditions as in new species discovered. The multifarious character of section IV was further illustrated by T. Wesley Mills, who after 1892 issued instalments of his investigations in animal psychology and intelligence. Devoted to the close observational methods of Darwin – one of his reports was a diary recording development of three litters of puppies – Mills abhorred the laboratory school, which he thought denied animals any reasoning power or memory. 'Let us have all the experiments possible – let us gather facts,' he wrote, 'let the facts be much more numerous than the theories, and let us be very cautious in drawing conclusions, especially such as seem to be radically destructive in tendency.'³ In their different spheres, Mills, Macoun, and Bell upheld a science devoted to observation and collection of facts, indeed identification of intellectual progress with the steady accumulation of facts.

Beginning in the early 1890s there crept into the scientific sections of the *Transactions* ever-increasing reference to research in laboratories. In 1891 George Lawson dismissively referred to mere collecting and naming specimens and pointed toward a new strategy for botany –

examination of the minute structure of plants and me-
tabolism and understanding the ways in which tissues
were modified by heat, light, moisture, and soil.[4] After
the turn of the century reports from university laboratories grew in profusion. Henry T. Bovey, founder of the
Faculty of Applied Science at McGill, conducted tests on
the strengths of Canadian timbers as construction materi-
als; his colleague Howard Barnes, the Macdonald Professor of Physics, examined the character of different types
of ice, a matter of considerable import given the potential
for hydro-electric power generation. From the physiologi-
cal laboratory at the University of Manitoba came accounts
of the effects of temperature changes on the life of the
frog and the influence of music – including the overture
to Wagner's *Tannhäuser* – on the blood pressure of humans.

The most wondrous reports of laboratory discoveries
came from Ernest Rutherford and his associates at McGill
on the nature of the atom and radiation. The physics
laboratory, which opened in 1893 and was funded by the
tobacco magnate Sir William Macdonald (who loathed
smoking), was one of the best equipped in the world, and
during Rutherford's stay there from 1898 to 1907 it was
at the forefront of a revolution in physics that involved
discovery of the electron, the concept of the atom as a
miniature solar system, and spontaneous disintegration
of certain elements, or radioactivity.[5] Rutherford made
known his important discoveries in British scientific journals, but those Canadians whom he inspired filled the
Transactions with their findings. Of 17 communications
from section III in 1911, eight dealt with radioactivity,
and these came not only from the McGill circle but also
from J.C. McLennan and his students at the University of
Toronto's physical laboratory.

The increasing prominence of laboratory reports was
accompanied by a self-conscious and determined quest
on the part of university-based researchers for greater public recognition and government support. Inspired by the

example of the German and American universities and by the Cavendish Laboratories at Cambridge, advocates of the research ideal campaigned for generous government funding of industrial and scientific research on many grounds, including utility. Deeply rooted in the notion of creating *new* knowledge was the sense of a conflict between the educational ideas implanted in Canada in the mid-nineteenth century and those brought back by Canadian and British academics who had studied in Germany and the United States. James Loudon, president of the University of Toronto, was scathing on this point: 'To hold up before students, either by theory or practice, solely the ideal of acquiring what has already been learned is mediaevalism pure and simple; it is to teach him to creep where he might might walk upright and alone; it is to rob him in part of that intellectual birthright of independent thought which is the inheritance of every man, at least since the Renaissance.' The research ideal was no less important for strengthening self-reliance in Canadian national life. 'The time has surely come,' Loudon declared, 'when we should cease to take all our knowledge at secondhand from abroad, and that we should do some original thinking suitable to our own circumstances.'[6]

This campaign for industrial and scientific research was promoted by the Canadian Manufacturers' Association, the Royal Canadian Institute, and individuals such as McLennan, and it succeeded in 1915 when the dominion government decided to set up the Honorary Advisory Council for Scientific and Industrial Research and gave this group – of the 11 members five were fellows of the Royal Society of Canada – control over funds for research grants and student awards. The Advisory Committee evolved into the National Research Council (NRC), which by 1932 possessed its own laboratories in Ottawa. NRC in effect became what the Royal Society had once aspired to be.

The War of 1914–18 accelerated these developments and generated what one scientist called a 'psychological condition'[7] favourable to research that was essential to defeat Germany, strengthen Canada's ability to withstand industrial competition after the struggle, and through planned development end wasteful destruction of natural resources. The decision to support scientific research was bound up with the war atmosphere in other, more subtle ways. The government that enforced conscription was an activist, reformist administration, which represented a widespread effort to transcend the old norms of politics and purify social relations through enfranchisement of women and prohibition. Conscription was strongly linked to a desire for British recognition of Canada's autonomy and to the feeling that Canada's new constitutional status implied that it cease being an 'intellectual parasite.'[8] In 1917 the biochemist A.B. Macallum, who headed the Advisory Council and was president of the Royal Society that year, observed that the war 'has made for the human race an almost complete break with the past' and that the future would bring 'a new world and a new age in which all the shibboleths will be discarded.' This was the language of wartime reformers in general, but Macallum saw the opportunities for change in terms of the age-long struggle between the old knowledge and the new. For too long classical studies and traditional learning had monopolized the intellectual world, and their prejudice against science had impeded its acceptance as an intellectual equal. For Macallum the 'new age' ushered in by the Great War and recognition that science should be supported for its contribution to military victory and industrial efficiency marked the beginning of its autonomy and equality,[9] a direct parallel to Canada's acquisition of autonomy and international recognition as a nation state.

For the society, the war years and the birth of the Advisory Council aggravated a long-standing publications problem. As far back as 1887 Lawson remarked on the preponderance of scientific papers over those in the liter-

- Send program to Michelle

-

    < VISITORS @ PENTICTON. ORG ?

Naramata
Lavender Lane Guest House
lavendarlane @ shaw. ca

Box ben vinyerds guest hous
uurs - BBCanada . com /
           Voxben

insurance — travel (
*? — house (locks?).

~~laundry~~

Call Johnnie + Caroline
~~Call Tommy~~
Email all contacts
Make up diary list of #s.
Money (balance) send Tessa's
cheque.

Write C + K

R.S.V.P.

WESTIN
HOTELS & RESORTS®

VISIT WESTIN.COM OR CALL 800-WESTIN1

ary and historical departments, and five years later Bourinot complained that the essays of sections I and II were 'literally buried' by a mass of scientific matter and urged unsuccessfully that the *Transactions* be split into two parts so that people interested in buying the literary articles need not purchase the entire volume.[10] The concern of scientists with publication was different; they protested that delay in issuing the annual report imperilled claims of priority and discouraged submission of important work. W. Lash Miller of the University of Toronto, who firmly believed that senior undergraduates should do research, took up the practice after 1902 of giving only highly condensed accounts of research in physical chemistry, assuring readers that the papers had already been published, or would very soon appear, in leading chemistry journals. 'Owing to the delay attending the publication of the Proceedings,' ran his reprimand, 'it has not been thought advisable to ask the Society to print these in full.'[11]

In 1905 the society encouraged publication of scientific papers during the year, and in 1914 it debated whether to print quarterlies for each section. This latter proposal was enthusiastically supported by section III, favoured in IV, and opposed by the literary and historical divisions. In 1915 three quarterlies – one for each of the science sections, and one for both sections I and II – appeared separately, members receiving copies of the proceedings of the society and the publication of the section to which they belonged. (The society reverted to a single volume in 1920, but after 1924 separate sectional instalments were the norm till after the Second World War.)

This was only part of the 'publications problem': the number of papers in the scientific sections – a new section V was created out of section IV in 1918 for the biological sciences – expanded in the postwar years. A considerable proportion of these pieces reported research funded by the Advisory Council, mainly in physics and chemistry.

This increase in research put pressure on the society's *Transactions*, the only Canadian medium for publication in these areas at a time when the government grant was cut to $3,000 in 1919. Even though the amount was restored to $8,000 in 1920 the society alone could not afford to publish even a fraction of the scientific papers. In the 1920s the NRC made grants ranging up from $750 to $3,000 a year to the society for publication of scientific reports, and universities contributed smaller amounts, from $500 from McGill and Toronto to half that figure from Dalhousie, Queen's, Manitoba, Saskatchewan, Alberta, and British Columbia, and, later, Laval.[12]

This febrile expansion of scientific reportage distended the *Transactions* to 1,640 pages by 1927, with sections I and II together accounting for 240; III, 506; IV, 242; and V, 538. Even so it was the frequent experience of section III particularly that only a portion of papers presented at meetings could be published. Of the 108 presentations in 1925 in physics and chemistry, 38 appeared in the *Transactions*. Only after creation of the *Canadian Journal of Research* under the auspices of the NRC in 1929 was some semblance of balance restored in the Royal Society's publication.

By this time the most striking features of the scientific sections was the growing importance of university research and the representation of academics in membership. Section IV lessened its dependence on the Geological Survey (which had 19 of 65 fellows); in section III, with 53 members, 17 were from the University of Toronto and 11 from McGill. Toronto came to dominate Canadian science in this period, with half of the 513 scientists trained in the country having been educated at that university.[13] There was a notable presence of scientists from the universities of Manitoba, Alberta, and British Columbia and a corresponding relative decline in numbers from the Maritimes. J.C. McLennan and his associates at Toronto reported con-

tinuously in the 1920s and early 1930s on electrical con-
ductivity of various substances at low temperatures; of
his lifetime output of some 250 articles about 85 appeared
in the *Transactions*, but not his famous discovery of the
Auroral green line, which was made known in the British
journal *Nature*.[14] In the 1920s the new biological section,
while still drawing on investigations sponsored by the
Biological Board, also reported many experiments following up the discovery at Toronto of insulin, which received
a Nobel prize in 1923, by J.J.R. Macleod, J.B. Collip, Charles
Best, and Frederick Banting. In 1923 section V published
28 papers, 10 related to insulin. In that decade John
Cameron of Dalhousie presented nearly thirty instalments
of his researches in craniometry – studies of facial aspects
of skulls – which had a direct bearing on divergences in
human evolution. None of these scientists experienced the
notoriety of E.L. Harrington, PhD, who scrutinized the
physics of curling stones and concluded that so long as
the ice was clean sweeping had no effect on the motion of
rocks. This paper was widely publicized and brought irate
criticism for years afterward.

The preponderance of membership in the society was shift-
ing to the scientists. Even before the Great War there were
57 fellows in sections I and II altogether and 75 in sections
III and IV. In the postwar years this proportion grew far
more unbalanced. The numbers in all sections were expanded, but by 1927 the science sections were limited only
by the restriction that no more than three new fellows
could be elected to any section in any single year. Thanks
to this rule, creation of section V, and the increase in limits
for sections I and II, by 1938 the society had 305 members, 200 of them in the science sections.[15] By that year
scientists were also further along the road to professional
status in so far as this was indicated by possession of a
doctorate. Forty-one of the 58 active fellows in the geo-

logical section had that degree; in section III, 52 of 80. The comparable figure for section II was 19 of 65, or less than one-third.

In the inter-war years scientists were in the forefront in advocating changes that would open up membership in the society. In 1923 section V proposed formation of a Canadian Association for the Advancement of Science – at the same time that l'Association Canadienne-française pour l'avancement des sciences (ACFAS) was being organized in Montreal – that would bring younger scientists into contact with their elders and with businessmen and the public generally. Section IV opposed this radical measure and suggested instead creation of an 'associate' membership which would preserve the principle of limited numbers of fellows and still improve the quality of meetings.[16] This idea resurfaced in the mid-1930s, when there was considerable agitation for enlarging representation of the 'social sciences.' In 1936 Lawrence J. Burpee, secretary of the society, canvassed opinions on the matter of associates and received replies from 141 of 300 fellows. Overall 91 approved the proposal, 38 were unfavourable, and 12 doubtful. Only in section I were the majority who replied opposed, and that section went on record as objecting strongly to so profound a change. Gustave Lanctot of the Public Archives told Burpee that 'the Royal Society has not been created to encourage young talents, ... but to consecrate past achievements and well-earned reputations ... It is a question of choice between the British principle of selection and the modern system of free-for-all mass meetings.'[17] Several of those who replied to Burpee felt that thanks to the actions of the science sections the total membership was too large and ought to be reduced. For Burpee, however, the idea of associate members was the only way of keeping the number of fellows down to a reasonable total by providing a category to which younger people could be elected. There were worries that the distinctions between 'associate' and 'Fellow' would be blurred and diminish the prestige of the latter; some people supported the new idea, provided that women were considered.

Robert W. Boyle of the NRC unburdened himself of a long-standing grievance of section III, which had advocated a separate section for chemistry since the early 1920s: 'It is quite wrong to include four great sciences i.e. Chemistry, Physics, Mathematics and Astronomy in one section, and leave the one science of Geology with a section all to itself. There are not many geologists in the country as compared with chemists, physicists and engineers, to say nothing of the mathematicians and astronomers. The inevitable and unfair consequence is that it is easier for a Geologist to be elected to a Fellowship.' Boyle was ready to abolish the sections altogether, except for purposes of program and publication.[18] The marine biologist A.G. Huntsman noted that there were two ideals in conflict – limited membership and bringing together all those doing valuable research work – but he was at a loss as to how to resolve the issue.[19] So was the society in general, for despite considerable support for associate membership nothing was decided. What is quite evident from the replies, however, was the determination of the fellows to preserve undiluted the prestige of their status in the society.

The scientific sections were more receptive to admission of women as members. Since the 1880s women had figured in the affairs of the society in a minor way through the reports of women's historical associations and in having their papers read to meetings by members. Among their contributions were studies of the outdoor and indoor games of the Wabanaki Indians, the history and civil rights of Canadian Jews, and the condition of the French-Canadian working class. None of these was printed in the *Transactions*, however, and the issue of female membership in the society did not arise till 1913, when – thanks to the efforts of J.G. Adami, who taught pathology at McGill,

R.F. Ruttan, director of the chemistry department there, and J.P. McMurrich, who taught anatomy at Toronto – the council agreed to interpret the word 'persons' in its by-laws as meaning individuals of either sex.[20] Nothing in effect changed until the growth in female enrolment in universities increased the number of reports from senior women students that were conveyed to the society by Lash Miller, J.C. McLennan, and others. A number of women had their research supported by the NRC. Among those who relied on the *Transactions* to bring out their findings were Carrie Derick of McGill, who had investigated the burnt-out districts of Saskatchewan in 1919, the plant pathologist Margaret Newton, who specialized in cereal rusts, and Alice Wilson of the Geological Survey, an expert on the fossils of the Ottawa Valley.

Membership, however, came with almost glacial speed. Alice Wilson was elected to section IV in 1938, Margaret Newton to V in 1942, the same year that Madeleine Fritz of the Royal Ontario Museum joined IV. Helen Hogg of the Dunlap Observatory near Toronto became a member of section III in 1946. It was not till 1947 that section I admitted the novelist Gabrielle Roy, and 1951 when section II elected Mabel Timlin, an economist from the University of Saskatchewan. This pace of change was protracted even by the Royal Society's standards and put it in the same league with arts faculties in the universities and the Anglican, though not the United Church, which ordained its first female minister in 1936.[21]

As its centre of gravity shifted to the science sections the society became dependent on the NRC for financing publications, and in 1932 – for its fifty-first meeting – it moved from the Victoria (or National) Museum to the new NRC building, where it would continue to convene for the next 35 years. Nineteen thirty-two marked the beginning of the second half-century of the society. (One member, W.L. Mackenzie King, however, thought so little of the occasion that he recorded in his diary two events of apparently equal significance: he registered at the Royal Society and bought some boxes of flowers and vegetables.)[22] The society commemmorated its anniversary with *Fifty Years Retrospect, 1882–1932*, a history with a purpose. It surveyed only lightly the evolution of the society as such, but the series of essays on the development of fields of study were offered as 'striking proof of the dominating part taken by the Fellows of the Royal Society in the intellectual and scientific life of the Dominion.' The society appropriated to itself some of the prestige of individual members for work that often had little to do with the organization as an institution.

Henry Marshall Tory, president of the NRC from 1928 to 1935, gave the society a room for an office and encouraged it to transfer its library to the NRC building as well. The society had collected some 21,000 volumes, the majority in the sciences, mainly through exchanges with other societies. It had stored these books and journals in the Victoria Museum, but in the early 1930s a committee decided that they served no useful purpose, given the society's scattered membership. In 1935 the scientific portion became part of the national scientific library of the NRC, which also stored the literary and historical works. Lawrence J. Burpee, who had been head of the Carnegie Library in Ottawa, voiced his displeasure in a curious turn of phrase. 'There are,' he said, 'still a few things that any self-respecting national learned society should possess – as a gentleman must wear clean linen, even though it cannot be proved useful – and among them are its *Transactions* and its Library.'[23] Burpee had a point: the library had always figured in the hope that the society would one day have its own building as headquarters, but as the economic depression deepened this seemed a very remote prospect. In a symbolic way, the transfer of the library to an institution it claimed to have helped create marked the point at which the society would begin to live in the NRC's shadow. In the mid-1940s the government grant to the society was placed in the estimates of the National Research Council.

The society's dependence on the NRC was only one part of its financial troubles in the inter-war years. Membership fees had increased in 1918 to $10 on election and $10 annually, but about 80 per cent of these revenues went towards travelling expenses of eligible members. The government grant fell from $8,000 in 1928 to $5,000 in 1933. The issue of creating an endowment was first raised in 1926 in the hope of securing permanent quarters in Ottawa. The next year the Carnegie Corporation of New York contributed $25,000 and the society resolved to raise a similar amount from its members, who pledged over $10,000 but actually turned over $3,655 by 1929. Some, then and later, were more generous than others. Judge Howay and A.H.R. Buller remembered the society in their wills – Howay left a legacy of $1,000 in 1945, Buller $12,000 in 1946 (after taxes, this latter amount was reduced to $9,838.44). The endowment campaign of the late 1920s was not a success, especially in regard to contributions from business. In 1929, before the effects of the Depression were felt, the Endowment Committee reported little progress and also that it had encountered an impression that was 'fairly widespread among leading business men in Canada that the Royal Society is an association of theorists discussing more or less abstruse problems.'[24] Part of the difficulty was judged to be lack of sufficient publicity about the activities of the society: one president had earlier remarked: 'Its existence is probably known in Ottawa, it is rumoured in Montreal, Toronto, Halifax, Winnipeg, but is it not practically unknown elsewhere?' In the late 1930s the council decided to pay a journalist – Wilfrid Eggleston – to cover a meeting in syndicated dispatches.[25] Two decades earlier it had been routine for the society at the close of its sessions to thank the local press for its full and sympathetic reports.

In 1939 the society presented a memorandum to the minister of finance requesting an increased grant on the grounds that the science sections in particular had been in the forefront of such discoveries as insulin and Marquis wheat but that the society could not afford to cover the printing expense with the current annual grant of $4,500. (After the Second War a note of petulance was evident in a similar request for increased funding: the society had not called itself into being, ran the claim, and the state had a contractual obligation to support its objectives.) At the same time that the society was protesting that it could no longer afford to print all the papers brought before it, the *Transactions* found considerable space for detailed coverage of a social event – an operetta-dinner in the ballroom of the Mount Royal Hotel that was paid for by the city of Montreal. The mayor, Camillien Houde, addressed the fellows but the *pièce de résistance* was a play written by the president, Victor Morin, a notary and authority on heraldry, who regreted deeply that their majesties, then on a Canadian tour, were unable to meet the society. The *Proceedings* for 1939 reprinted the menu, listing the courses and the verses that were sung to the accompaniment of each, as well as the dramatis personae.[26]

There were two advances related to finance that were more encouraging. First, in the late 1920s the society was finally able to make awards in recognition of intellectual merit. These medals, endowed by the millionaire meat packer Joseph Flavelle, Lorne Pierce, and the geologist J.B. Tyrrell, were established to reward outstanding achievement in, respectively, science (1925); imaginative and creative writing, with priority given to Canadian literature (1926); and Canadian history (1928). These medals were open to all, but there was a tendency to bestow them on members of the society, which is understandable, given its success in electing creative people as well as the relatively small Canadian intellectual community. In 1926 the Flavelle medal went to J.C. McLennan

(W. Lash Miller waited till 1938), and the Pierce medal to the poet Charles G.D. Roberts. Adjutor Rivard, philologist of the French language in Canada, received the Pierce medal in 1931. Women writers were recognized long before they were admitted to section II: the Pierce medal was given to Mazo de la Roche in 1938, Dorothy Livesay in 1947, and Gabrielle Roy in 1948. The citation for Livesay made clear that her poetry was considered on aesthetic grounds regardless of her 'proletarian enthusiasms.'[27] Margaret Newton received the Flavelle medal in 1948.

The second development resulted from the contacts with the Carnegie Corporation. In 1931 the corporation allotted $15,750 annually for five years to endow 10 research scholarships of $1,500 each for Canadian students, to be administered by the society. The Carnegie directors originally thought of the fellowships as being only for the sciences and administered by the NRC; L.J. Burpee and the council intervened and changed this approach.[28] The society decided that two of these fellowships would be given in each of the five general subject areas represented by the sections; in 1934 the rule was altered to one each, with the remaining five given at the discretion of the fellowships board.

Known as the Royal Society of Canada Fellowships, these awards were intended to support post-graduate training and research abroad and they were open to both sexes. In 1932 there were some 140 applications (27 from women), and these figures indicate the fields of graduate study that were popular at that time: French literature and philosophy (8), geology (10), chemistry and physics (11 each), biology (13), and history and literature (13 each), economics (15). In 1937 financing was renewed on a diminishing scale; by 1943, when it was considered undesirable to continue because of the war, some $134,100 in Canadian funds had been dispensed by the Carnegie Corporation (the society that year returned $12,948.66.)[29]

The impact of these fellowships would become clear

only in the future: students in the humanities who were helped included A.G. Bailey, Earle Birney, J. Roy Daniels, J.-C. Falardeau, H. Northrop Frye (for a study of symbolism in the prophetic books of William Blake), Thomas Goudge, Alice Jean Lunn, and G.F.G. Stanley. When the society had decided to take on management of the scheme it was said: 'If it does not add much to the dignity and prestige of the Society, at least it will not detract from them.'[30] In light of the preceding names this venture deserves higher marks. (In the postwar years the fellowship scheme was reactivated with monies from the provinces and the federal government.) Up to 1949 the Carnegie Corporation had given the Royal Society $163,000 for its endowment and the scholarships – a minuscule portion of the $6 million that it made available to Canadian educational institutions in the first half of the century.[31]

4

Relations between the
Humanities and the Sciences

By the 1930s there was a growing impression among more
reflective fellows that members of the Royal Society had
lost a sense of the institution as a whole and that interchanges among the sections, including the scientific and
literary departments, were insubstantial. But this had not
always been the case: indeed, during the first generation
of the society sectional boundaries were porous to a degree and there existed significant links, affinities, and cross-
overs between the scientific and literary groups. It has
already been pointed out that there was a close parallel in
the procedures of the naturalists in establishing facts and
the determination of historical writers to draw out details
from documentary sources in a scientific spirit.

It was possible also in the early years for James LeMoine,
an ornithologist as well as a chronicler of legendary lore,
to publish papers in three of the four sections and for
George M. Dawson to deliver his presidential address to
section IV on the geology of the Rocky Mountains and the
next year publish in Section II notes on the Shuswap people
of British Columbia. Another geologist, J.B. Tyrrell, who
made his reputation with a strenuous trek across the bar-
ren lands and the discovery of dinosaur remains in the
Red Deer Valley of Alberta, grew to admire the exploits
of the explorer-surveyor David Thompson, whose journal
he edited and whose work he tirelessly memorialized.

The Laval geologist J.C.K. Laflamme examined the annals of earth tremors in Quebec dating back to the seventeenth century and wrote appreciatively of Michael Sarrazin and his place in the history of science in Canada. The botanist David Penhallow of McGill described predecessors in the field in a thorough fashion in articles that were on a par with those by the historical writers of the time. From another angle, Samuel E. Dawson, in trying to establish the routes of Cabot and Cartier, supplemented the laconic documents with information then being recorded by the survey of tides and currents in Canadian waters.

Some members of the humanities section were thoroughly immersed in scientific subjects, especially botany, in the course of their intellectual development. Adam Shortt painted flowers and taught chemistry and botany at Queen's before turning to economic history, and Léon Gérin was a devoted botanist who proceeded to Paris to study the subject further but was diverted into social studies. In Shortt's detailed chronicle of Canadian banks and in Gérin's precise inventory of the possessions of the habitant families of Saint-Justin there were signs of the botanist's zest for concreteness and exactitude. E.Z. Massicotte was an equally dedicated botanist and friend of Marie-Victorin, the priest who popularized the subject in Quebec in the inter-war years.

The most outstanding instance of the cross-over between science and history in the Royal Society, however, was the case of William Francis Ganong, who was born in New Brunswick and returned there each summer to explore its natural and human history and who taught botany at Smith College in Massachusetts. Ganong held a Munich PhD and carried out researches in plant physiology; he also aspired to write a comprehensive history of his native province that would integrate all that could be known about its physiography, natural history, Aboriginal peoples, European settlements, place names, boundaries, and maps. He realized early on that such a study in his hands would lack life and form, and instead he published in the *Transactions* from the 1880s into the 1930s a succession of monographs on virtually all these subjects. Ganong's approach to history was in the spirit of exact scientific analysis and analogy. 'Place names,' he explained in 1896, 'form a permanent register or index of the course and events of a country's history; they are the fossils exposed in the cross-section of that history, marking its successive periods.' He pointed also to the striking parallels between evolution in nature and the development of maps. 'One who knows something of the influences at work in organic evolution may here find parallels with curious and often startling exactness, the familiar phenomena of variation, adaptation and survival of the fittest. He can see heredity, the old features, coming into conflict with new knowledge, representative of environment, and the result of the struggle is always a compromise, as it is in Nature.'[1] Though such general considerations lay back of Ganong's studies his friend J.C. Webster isolated the chief feature of his work: Ganong was 'essentially a fact-finder ... He never indulged in the misdemeanor of filling hiatuses with fanciful imaginings.'[2] For over fifty years Ganong's pieces appeared in the *Transactions* relentlessly, making him without doubt the single most published contributor to its pages.

Beyond these points of contact between scientific and historical writers were general and disturbing issues associated with science. The Royal Society was founded in the year Charles Darwin died, and none of the early members could have been unaware of the controversies over evolution through natural selection and its application to human origins. Both William Dawson and Daniel Wilson had expended considerable energy in engaging Darwin's ideas. Dawson had issued many semi-popular tracts denouncing Darwin's unwarranted hypothetical argument and pointing to the lack of geological evidence for transmutation;

Wilson was more open-minded and accommodating, but he could not bring himself to believe that humanity's higher attributes had been produced by material nature alone. Within the society Dawson exercised self-restraint in not raising these issues, even though Chauveau remarked that the society was fortunate in having as its first president a person (Dawson) who insisted on religion in science. In his presidential address in 1886 Wilson mentioned how Darwin's hypothesis had affected scientific work in geology, palaeontology, and psychology and saw these 'speculations' increasingly converging on questions affecting humanity. It was well to remember, he counselled, that evolution – a hypothesis that had become a dogma – necessarily pointed to a beginning, a creator.[3]

The very coupling of the sciences with belles-lettres in the organization of the society evoked uneasy feelings among those who identified science only with painstaking observation. Mgr Thomas E. Hamel taught the subject at Laval and was fully aware of the obstacles to the pursuit of the sciences in Quebec; the cause of science, he felt, was hardly enhanced by its contamination with materialism and unbelief. Thus in his president's addresses to section III and to the society at large he criticized evolution on many grounds and dismissed Darwinism as 'une pure hypothèse fantaïsiste.' Abbé Casgrain said of Herbert Spencer's cosmic evolution that it was a cult of materialism that made paganism seem filled with spiritual life.[4]

Within the society such observations on evolution were untypical. Scientists avoided commenting on the general theory and confined their references to Darwin to specific observations, as did Penhallow in an article on movements in plants. This circumspection was the case even with such controversialists as William LeSueur, who had defended evolution and the positive aspects of modern thought so vigorously that it has been speculated that his entry into the society was delayed for that reason.[5] (This determination to avoid controversy, however, did not inhibit Archbishop O'Brien of Halifax from defending miracles – the intervention of the Divine Being in the ordinary course of events – as compatible with natural law; or William Bell Dawson, William's son and a chip off the old block, who discoursed on solar and lunar cycles deduced from the Book of Daniel.) It was not till the fiftieth anniversary of the publication of Darwin's *Origin of Species* in 1909 that the society was treated to a general appraisal of the secure status of evolution in scientific circles.[6]

Yet in the mid-1920s, when efforts were being made in a few American states to prohibit the teaching of evolution in the schools, the geologist W.A. Parks returned to the subject and testified that among the scientifically trained there was a profound conviction of the truth of the doctrine of organic evolution. Still,

We know practically nothing of the nature of life. On secular evidence alone, we know not whence it came, what purpose it serves, or what destiny awaits it in the future ... That life is no more than a physico-chemical process, proceeding without design, and tending to no objective, is a materialistic conception that I am utterly unable to accept. I believe that God created life on the globe an immensity of time ago and endowed it with the power of development that has expressed itself in what we call evolution. I believe that this development has proceeded in obedience to His laws to the fulfillment of His Divine Purpose.[7]

Park's attestation would have brought nods of approval from William Dawson, and Wilson and Hamel too.

The relations of the scientific and literary cultures came in for explicit comment in numerous presidential addresses. Samuel Dawson in 1908 conceded the bias of the age toward the sciences and drew a sharp distinction between the two realms. 'The spheres of Science and Literature, though they seem at times to coalesce,' he explained, 'are profoundly diverse. The former is fundamentally quantitative – the latter is radically qualitative.' Science dealt with material forms and forces, with numbers, weights, and measures; literature (and here he included history, economics, political studies) took as its sphere the moral and intellectual forces and the constants in human nature and behaviour. 'The laws of conduct,' he wrote, pointing to the recent revolution in the understanding of the atom, 'have been more stable than the theories of the constitution of matter.'[8] This conceit – that classical studies and literature were superior to science – was reinforced during the Great War, when science's claims for greater recognition were being identified with the war aims of the Allies.

In 1915 Maurice Hutton, who taught classics at Toronto, spoke on Thucydides and history, and his ruminations alluded frequently to the war in progress. Hutton's writings were impressionistic, elliptical, and invariably illustrated a moral lesson with reference to classical literature. Knowledge to him was more than information or mastery of a 'subject'; it involved an insight into human nature and conduct and a spiritual reality beyond the reach of science that could be understood intuitively. Hutton detested 'research' inspired by the procedures of science, fragmentation of learning, and especially those historians who subordinated personality and human agency to economic forces. Reflecting on Thucydides and war, Hutton wrote: 'Science can do much in warfare – especially in modern warfare – but it cannot supply energy. It may easily diminish the energy of native will and natural force of character.'[9]

It was not lost on Hutton or on Robert Falconer, who was president of his university, that the claims advanced by those such as Macallum involved adoption of German methods to defeat the enemy. In a comparison of educational ideas illuminated by the conflict Falconer equated German militarism with a discipline and habit of mind that exalted the state, organization, and science and contrasted this with the French tradition of producing citizens, not specialists.[10] Hutton and Falconer were among the last of the Victorian idealists, but their attitudes to science were shared by other classicists who would fight a rearguard action in the universities for two decades after the war. (Oddly, as the prestige of classics declined the numbers of papers on Greece and Rome in the *Transactions* increased: in the period 1882–1930 there were eight; in the following 30 years, 47.)[11]

Hutton's sentiments were not out of harmony with the feelings of others in section II. James Cappon, Stephen Leacock, Andrew Macphail, and George Wrong also disdained German-inspired American scholarship and lamented the subdividing of knowledge into ever-smaller compartments. Cappon, who taught English at Queen's and saw his position as that of a lonely apostle of culture in a backwater, was less tactful than the rest in dismissing the Physics Building at his university as merely a place 'having glass bottles with wires in them' and calling his colleagues who worked there '"educated plumbers" with a slight hesitation on the first word.'[12] With a biting satire Leacock paid his respects in *Arcadian Adventures with the Idle Rich* (1914) to the new educational order represented by Plutoria University, with its largest buildings housing the faculties of industrial and mechanical science, a university that taught everything – forestry, dentistry, palmistry – and whose press 'sent out a shower of bulletins and monographs like driven snow from a rotary plough.'[13]

This conservative strain, and not only in relation to the sciences, was prevalent in other quarters of section II. When G.M. Grant said back in 1891 that this section had been in a 'state of anaemia' he meant that it had not really addressed its mandate of cultivating English literature, and he therefore supported the addition of members who taught that subject in schools and colleges.[14] This end was partially accomplished with election of Duncan Campbell Scott, a poet as well as an administrator, Cappon, Pelham Edgar of Victoria College, Toronto, and Herbert L. Stewart, who taught philosophy at Dalhousie and founded the *Dalhousie Review* in 1921. Edgar and Stewart wrote a species of literary appreciation and intellectual history that engaged a writer's ideas and not infrequently used them to launch darts at the foibles of their own time. With Edgar's studies of Matthew Arnold, Henry James, and Shelley and Stewart's essays on Carlyle, Shaw, and Tolstoy, the range of section II was extended considerably beyond the Canadian confines.

These two writers and Duncan Campbell Scott sensed a great disjunction between the pre- and postwar years, a break expressed at one level by assaults on 'Victorianism' and 'Puritanism,' which came to stand for something prim if not repressive, and at another by abandonment of the standards, both in culture and comportment, of their own generation. In his presidential address of 1922 Scott almost ritualistically compared section II, with its varied subject matter, to the scientific sections, which 'have an advantage over us in that they have greater solidarity of aim, that their groups have clearly defined objects of study and investigation, and their results are more tangible.' 'Letters,' he said 'will always envy Science its busyness with material things.'

It was not science, at least not directly, that exercised Scott, however, but the 'revolt against established forms ... This is a critical age and it has a peculiar tone of criticism. Compared with other times it more loudly and insistently questions and mocks at the past.' It seemed to him that the purpose of the new criticism was not so much to create beauty 'as to insult older ideas of beauty ... to mock with unwholesome audacities.'[15] Edgar returned to this latter point and condemned the literary modernity of 'the spurious type that reacts with revolutionary violence against accepted forms.' One facet of this rebellion that he (and Scott) found particularly objectionable was the popularity of Freudianism and psychoanalysis. 'You are not permitted to love your mother without wishing to marry her and cut your father's throat, and aberrations of your maturity are explicable in terms of some pre-natal discontent.' The preoccupation with sex and erotic frankness, both by critics who searched out complexes and perversions in the literature of the past and by such contemporary novels as D.H. Lawrence's *Sons and Lovers*, Edgar wrote, may be a reaction to the excessive reticence of the preceding age, but it presented a very unbalanced view of life.

As for Freudianism as a science, according to Edgar, it originated in a study of abnormal types in the most sex-ridden city of Europe, and its future would, he hoped, be short. 'For a long time our novelists flew the banner of Evolution. Heredity, environment and determinism were the accredited forerunners of the complexes, inhibitions, and sublimations of our more enlightened day.' Literary evaluation should not attach itself to a theory in the process of disintegration, the most recent phase of the wrong-headed borrowings from science. 'Judgement and experience can reach the springs of conduct without the aid of any mechanical instrument.'[16]

Stewart was more hospitable to Freudianism; indeed he thought that only attention to the latent content of Tolstoy's ideas could adequately explain a profound change in his temperament. 'There is,' he admitted, 'a great deal of unmapped country within us which would have to be taken into account in an explanation of our gusts and storms.' Yet he too lamented the declining reputation of the Victorian sages, notably Carlyle, and the tendency of modern critics to sneer at his 'Kaiser-Worship' and his negative attitudes to political economy and the social sciences. 'The old critics used to assume that it was Carlyle's greatness rather than his littleness which concerned mankind. The new critics assume the reverse.'[17]

The one scholar in section II who was acutely aware of the 'need for reuniting Science and the humanities,' George S. Brett, who taught philosophy at Toronto, was singularly well equipped to comment on the subject. Between 1912 and 1921 he published three volumes on the history of psychology in which he traced changing concepts of human nature from antiquity and paid close attention to the ways in which science figured in the story. In 1919 he invited the fellows to consider the contemporary revolt against reason on many levels, the most troubling of which were the conclusions of science. What place has reason in modern life in the light of the emphasis that physiology and biology had placed on reflexes, hereditary tendencies, 'even hereditary memories,' or the notion of 'the unconscience' or evolution, which exhibited humanity as 'genetically a monkey'?

For Brett the teachings of science were bound up with an old conflict of 'classics' versus 'moderns,' 'a struggle between two ideals of life and two types of civilization.' These might be bridged, he thought, by a history of science that treated it as a social product. One result of the highly technical character of modern science was the tendency to ignore the organic relations of science and the totality of human life. A history that was more sociology than past politics would reveal to scientists that they were not independent of social forces; it would also bring into the open and neutralize the causes of the opposition to science.[18]

In 1940 H.M. Tory, who was fascinated by the history of science, remarked on this 'cleavage of interest between science and the humanities' and affirmed: 'Science is dealing mainly with the external world of matter; literature mainly with the internal world of the spirit. The point of contact between them is that both these worlds belong to nature and each in its own field of activity is constantly using both method and knowledge derived from the other.' Both were reactions of mind to the universe and could not be antagonistic. Tory suggested that the society should have each year a major symposium of the sections and urged two possible topics: the effect of science on literature and the present state of the controversy between science and philosophy.[19]

Though Brett and Tory were examples of thinking beyond sectional divisions, nothing came of their recommendations.

5

The Rise of the Social Sciences

The members of the Royal Society encountered science in another guise – the 'social sciences.' This phrase entered the discourse of the society in the decade before the Great War, and by the late 1930s, when its supporters were advocating more adequate representation, the social sciences contained a cluster of subjects, the most prominent of which were political economy and a type of history closely allied to it, as well as anthropology, political science, psychology, and sociology.

It was already clear in 1908 that the subject divisions set out in 1882 could no longer contain either new fields or the expansion of old ones. Proposals were afoot to split section IV into two sections, one for geology and mineralogy, and another for biological sciences (which was done in 1918). Questions were asked as to what section geography belonged to. And in 1908 two members of section I – Léon Gérin and Errol Bouchette – urged a new section for the social sciences.

Léon Gérin, a nephew of Benjamin Sulte, worked in Ottawa first as a ministerial secretary and from 1882 to 1936 as translator of debates for the House of Commons. After the usual education in classical studies and law Gérin had gone to Paris in 1885 to pursue his real interest in botany; there he discovered the Ecole de la science sociale

of Edmond Demolins and abbé Henri de Tourville, who
applied the teachings of Frédéric LePlay to exact observation of human society, especially the family. Gérin carried
over into his examination of habitant families and classification of social groups something of the botanist's concern with minute observation and categorizing. His
'L'Habitant de Saint-Justin' (1898), a study of 222 families
in his uncle's parish, described the rural household in
terms of cattle and crops, size of farms, equipment and
methods of agriculture, women's work, diet, domestic
utensils, life cycles, wills and inheritance practices, and
figures of authority in the community. Gérin pursued social types back into the French regime and attributed the
failure to develop industry partially to the military ethos
of the colony and to dependence on public office, in contrast to the English seaboard colonies, where private initiative and individualism prevailed. (Demolins had attributed the later superiority of Anglo-Saxons in this regard
to their educational systems.)

For Gérin 'sociology' or social science was simply the
extension of scientific methods to the scrutiny of groups
and social institutions; in explaining the subject, however,
and in popularizing it he confronted a suspicion of social
science that stemmed from Comte's rejection of religion,
the materialism of Marx and Engels, and doubts about
science as such. Thus in his general surveys of the nature
of the subject he emphasized that it was in accord with
Catholic theology and that priests were active in promoting sociological studies. Sociology, moreover, offered to
Gérin a corrective to the unbalanced intellectual preoccupations of his compatriots, who he believed exaggerated
language and religion at the expense of the economic and
material foundations of their nationality.[1] Gérin's defence
of sociology was tactically similar to Hamel's effort to
justify the observational sciences against Darwinian fan-
tasies, or for that matter Laurier's attempt to distinguish
British liberalism from the European, anti-clerical type.

Gérin's fellow civil servant Errol Bouchette of the Library of Parliament had attempted at the turn of the century to explain the reasons for French-Canadian economic inferiority and called for reforms to the educational system that would place more emphasis on professional schools, technical education, and the applied sciences. The key to these changes was the study of political economy. Like Gérin, Bouchette and, later, Edouard Montpetit, who taught economics at the Ecole des hautes études commerciales after 1910, argued that the study of material life was essential in the interests of French-Canadian self-reliance and survival.[2] The new subjects were thus made compatible with traditional values. Indeed when Gérin was honoured in 1941 by the Royal Society with the Lorne Pierce medal for his contribution to Canadian literature the citation mentioned especially his appreciation for the nobility, beauty, and simplicity of rural life and treated his works as precursors of Louis Hémon's *Marie Chapdelaine*.[3]

In 1908 Bouchette argued that, in light of the large influx into Canada of British as well as non-traditional immigrants and the need to survey and describe the various groups, a new section of the society be created for 'Social Science and Economics.' This proposal was rejected, but the fields of both sections I and II were extended to 'French [or English] Literature, Archaeology, Sociology, Political Economy and Allied Subjects.' In 1912 section I voted to change 'Allied Subjects' to 'science moral et politique,' but the general designation remained. As often in the history of the Royal Society the solution to this problem also involved expansion of numbers in the two language sections.

While Bourinot had made a case for the study of political science in Canadian universities as early as 1889, some thirty years later there were only five 'social scientists' among the 35 fellows in section II. They were separated from the historians more by the subject matter they studied and their aspirations than by their methods. Adam Shortt had explored the origins of the Canadian banking system, and in the 23-volume *Canada and Its Provinces* (1913–17), which he edited with Arthur Doughty, he made sure that economic development, transportation, and tariffs were accorded adequate space. James Mavor of Toronto was an authority on the economic history of Russia, and Mackenzie King, elected in 1910 and for some time the only member of the section with a PhD, was well known for his efforts at conciliation in industrial relations and as deputy minister of labour. Stephen Leacock, who taught political economy at McGill and had written a widely read text in political science, was, like Shortt, a frequent contributor to university periodicals on current issues, in Leacock's case the *University Magazine*, edited by his friend Andrew Macphail, in Shortt's *Queen's Quarterly*. When Leacock, Mavor, and Shortt, and others organized the short-lived Canadian Political Science Association in 1913 they declared it to be 'the outcome of the widespread conviction that changing times have brought both the need and the possibility of more systematic investigation and discussion of our political, economic and social issues.'[4] These changing times had much to do with the acceleration of economic and urban growth, industrialization, and rapid settlement of western Canada in the preceding 15 years. Such social issues as urban congestion, child welfare, and non–Anglo-Saxon immigration were taken up by reformers within the Protestant denominations who were leaders in popularizing sociology and undertaking community surveys. Sociology was closely allied to social work and social betterment. One of the first sociologists appointed to a university department was an ordained Baptist minister who had been trained at Chicago – Carl Dawson, at McGill in 1922.[5]

This growing awareness of the importance of economic and social developments linked some members of the society to the many-sided progressive reform movement of the 1880–1920 period. Encompassing moral uplift and social purity as well as determination to apply a scientific approach to social and economic problems – even a 'scientific tariff' – this reformist thrust was most evident in the society's endorsement of conservation or the efficient use of natural resources, in the self-confidence of advocates of government support of scientific research in the interest of industrial efficiency and, later, war, and in smaller matters, as when a biologist urged consideration of eugenics as a basis for a more selective immigration policy. Such was the promise of science and scientific method that they were equated by some reformers with control, order, and rational management. Advocates of the 'social sciences' carried over not a little of this faith in advancing the claims of themselves and their subjects.

In actuality, there was an indistinctness about the concept of the social sciences in the 1920s that contrasts sharply with the precision associated with the word 'science.' It is highly unlikely that Leacock would have described himself as a scientist, for, in addition to being a humorist who respected the variety of human nature as it was, he thought of economics as a bundle of half-truths and oversimplifications. He gave two papers to section II on the position and outlook of political economy and on the grain of truth in popular economic fallacies, neither of which was published. Mavor thought it an outrage that Leacock's observations were so lacking in the fundamental principles of economic science; as an opponent of state interference in the economy, he must have been equally irritated by Leacock's *Unsolved Riddle of Social Justice* (1920), which summoned governments to support social security measures. Leacock was hardly a zealous promoter of 'social science' in the society; in fact he rarely attended meetings, and the section deliberated more than once whether to put him on the retired list. In 1928 he published in the *Transactions* a curious study on the economic importance of civil aviation, which began – 'My own experience as an aviator is limited to one brief, and absolutely final flight' – and then descended into a profusion of statistics on routes, freight carried, and accidents, almost a parody of social science reportage. While this contribution seemed to have made up for his past delinquencies, in 1932 he suddenly resigned on grounds of personal economy. B.K. Sandwell, who had briefly taught economics with Leacock at McGill but was better known as the editor of *Saturday Night*, said that Leacock's interest in the Royal Society and other learned bodies was seriously impaired because those organizations met at a time of year when the fishing in Lake Couchiching was excellent. Leacock was 'a devoted Fellow and took a lively interest in all that part of the Society's work which does not require attendance in May and June.'[6]

For all his idiosyncrasies Leacock up to a point shared the desire for involvement in public questions and current affairs that was so pronounced among social scientists. They envisaged themselves as experts who possessed special knowledge and aspired to become advisers to governments, just as natural scientists had been recruited earlier into the Experimental Farm or the Commission of Conservation. Shortt had served on the Civil Service Commission and on many boards and voluntary groups, and his most promising student and colleague, O.D. Skelton, became under-secretary of state in the Department of External Affairs. Ottawa had recognized the need for collection of information and in 1918 created the Dominion Bureau of Statistics under Robert H. Coats. The economist Duncan MacGibbon worked for the Board of Grain Commissioners.

The potential role of social scientists was expanded in the economic collapse of the 1930s when many looked to government initiative and economic expertise to institute planning and restore a sense of direction. This was the case with those who advocated Keynesian fiscal policy and the welfare state as well as those to their left who embraced programs of extensive nationalization and state intervention. The central position of the economists especially was indicated by the revival of the Canadian Political Science Association in 1929 and the founding of the *Canadian Journal of Economics and Political Science* in 1934. By 1942 the association had 900 members even though no more than 140 were political economists and historians in universities – a small fraction of an estimated 2,661 professors and college principals in the country.[7]

While a relatively small group, social scientists were self-confident and shared a conviction that their subject had come into its own. They wrote 11 background reports for the Rowell-Sirois Commission on Dominion-Provincial Relations, 1937–40, and were heavily involved in two major collaborative research projects – the eight-volume Frontiers of Canadian Settlement series, 1934–7, edited by William A. Mackintosh of Queen's, and a 26-volume series on the relations of Canada and the United States, published 1936–45 under the auspices of the Carnegie Endowment for International Peace.

During the late 1930s steps were taken to organize a committee that would bring researchers in the social sciences into closer contact. Conceived by Coats, and vigorously promoted by the economic historian Harold Innis of Toronto and the historian Reginald Trotter of Queen's, the Canadian Social Science Research Council (CSSRC) was formed in 1940 and was able in its early years to support research and subsidize publication of books using funds from the Carnegie and Rockefeller foundations. (Formation of this council was encouraged by the Canadian Historical Association, the Canadian Political Science Association, and the Royal Society of Canada, which altogether gave the founders a grant of $40 in 1938.) The CSSRC paid the expenses for the organizational meetings of a group chaired by the classicist Watson Kirkconnell that included A.S.P. Woodhouse of Toronto and Maurice

Lebel, a classicist from Laval, which eventually established the Humanities Research Council of Canada in 1943.[8]

The rise of the social sciences was connected with two other changes in the intellectual landscape that affected the Royal Society as an institution. The first was the appearance after 1920 of such specialized organizations as the Canadian Historical Association and the Canadian Political Science Association and such bodies as the Canadian Institute of International Affairs and the League of Nations Society, which were devoted to cultivating informed public opinion on Canada's external relations. The Carnegie Series in Canadian-American relations was accompanied by conferences that attracted nearly every Canadian social scientist and historian. Outlets for publication also increased in the period, ranging from the bumptious and nationalist *Canadian Forum* (1920) and staid *University of Toronto Quarterly* (1931) to the semi-popular *Canadian Geographic Journal* (1930).

There was considerable overlapping of membership in these associations and involvement with these publications. Lawrence J. Burpee, who was the Royal Society's secretary for a decade after 1926 offers a modest illustration. He was Canadian secretary of the International Joint Commission, which advised the governments of Canada and the United States on boundary waters, and his avocation was the history of early exploration, which brought him into contact with Innis and Frank Roe, whose works he introduced to the society. He was a staunch advocate of a national library and fond of saying that Canada, like Siam and Abyssinia, was unusual in not having one. Burpee was a founder and first editor of the *Canadian Geographic Journal*, one-time president of the Canadian Historical Association, and head of the Ottawa branch of the Canadian Institute of International Affairs. Such examples of loyalties beyond the society could be multiplied: the society increasingly became only one of many points of contact for individuals in a national network of writers, social scientists, and other intellectuals and for most not the most important one.[9]

The relative status of section II in particular was further diminished by the resolute apoliticism of most of its members and their determination to stand above contention and politics. Yet the 1930s was an intensely political, questioning decade, and the section seemed indifferent to this mood. In fact one might read through the *Transactions* of this period and remain almost oblivious to the collapse of the Canadian economy or of even darker developments elsewhere. It was typical of the society that it should turn down an invitation in 1938 from the secretary of the League of Nations Society in Canada to be represented on the National Committee on Refugees and Victims of Political Persecution on the grounds that 'this question has no connection with the activities of the Royal Society.'[10] Indeed it had none, but that is not the point. For those who were concerned about the rise of fascism, the threat of war, and economic reconstruction the society seemed timorous and remote.

The second development that affected the Royal Society was the efflorescence of a kind of Canadian historical writing that was quite different from the constitutional studies of the 1920s as well as the tradition of discrete, localistic, and documentary articles exemplified by Judge Howay's lists of trading vessels. The new history owed much to Harold Innis, whose *Fur Trade in Canada* (1930) inspired a type of economic history that aimed at establishing general patterns and dynamics in Canadian development with particular reference to resource industries and a type of history that was more attentive to economic forces and motives. The historical studies of Donald Creighton, Arthur Lower, and William Mackintosh stood in striking contrast to the tendency of historians in both language sections to perpetuate a seeming antiquarianism. It was not merely their suspicion of generalizations or the fact that many were 'amateurs' that appeared out-moded: it was their intense localism, which contrasted so sharply with the thrust of the new history towards an integrated national perspective that presented the history of Canada as more than the collection of isolated localities.

The key figure in these changes was Harold Innis of the Political Economy Department at Toronto, which, with 14 members in 1939, was the largest in the country. Innis was zealous in advancing the social sciences in Canada on many fronts, including the Royal Society. Elected in 1934, he was in some respects out of sympathy with its conventions. He told Burpee in 1936 that in nominations too much attention was paid to personalities and geography and not enough to the calibre of the work done.[11] That was what one might expect from Toronto – rejection of the custom running back to the earliest days of the society of trying to ensure regional and provincial representation.

In 1939 Innis resigned from section II and asked that his name be placed on the retired list as a protest against the awarding of the Lorne Pierce medal for distinction in Canadian literature to Wilfred Bovey for *The French Canadian To-day* (1938). Bovey had been given honorary degrees by Laval and Montréal and made a member of the Légion d'honneur. The Royal Society's citation, prepared by jurist Edouard Fabre Surveyer, the only French-Canadian member of section II, praised his book for predicting the visit of the king, the European crisis, and the government's policy regarding conscription, and generally for promoting the *entente cordiale* between the two peoples. Innis thought the award the result of French-Canadian influence, and while he conceded that the book might merit attention as a contribution to better understanding he did not consider it exactly what Pierce had in mind when the medal was established.[12] (Innis might also have been thinking of some of the 120 more important books that appeared in the decade in social sciences and history.) The storm passed, and he was reinstated the next year, became vice-president of section II in 1941, and was elected president of the society in 1947.

The solution to the problem of accommodating the social sciences within the society was, as usual in its affairs, long drawn out. The case made for a separate section by Bouchette in 1908 was reiterated by the historian William Grant in 1919 and by Burpee in 1925. Burpee characterized section II as heterogeneous and unwieldy and suggested dividing it in two – one part to embrace history, literature, and possibly philosophy, the other economics, anthropology, and similar subjects. (This proposal was, incidentally, supported by section III, which had its own interest in setting precedents for further subdivisions.) In 1932 both section II and council went on record as favouring division of that section into IIA – English, Philosophy, Languages and Allied Subjects – and IIB – English History, Archaeology, Sociology, Political Economy, and Allied Subjects. (In 1933 geography was grouped in the geological section.) By 1936 little in fact had changed: of the 64 members of section II no more than five could be considered active social scientists – Innis and E.J. Urwick from Toronto, Mackintosh, Coats, and R. MacGregor Dawson, a political scientist then at the University of Saskatchewan.

In 1940 H.M. Tory, who took more than a passing interest in the affairs of the society as a whole, saw the problem of finding a place for the social sciences as an extension of the older conflict that had pitted traditional learning against the sciences. 'Indeed,' he remarked, 'it is not unusual to hear members of Sections III, IV and V of our own Society speak of some of the subjects mentioned as having no right to the word 'science' and little right to membership in this learned body.' We should be prepared, he advised, to recognize new forms of knowledge as they arise.[13] In the same year, Arthur Beauchesne, who had succeeded to Bourinot's post as clerk to the House of Commons, advocated a drastic step by which this could be done – amalgamation of sections I and II into a new section I which would confine itself to literature, philosophy, and certain aspects of history in both French and English, leaving section II to develop the social sciences. Section I rejected this plan outright; section II also resolved to remain intact, with the option of dividing into two subsections. (These proposals were bound up with the debate over 'associate' members and, to a lesser degree, suggestions for admitting female members.)

Only in 1941 was the matter settled – again by expanding the membership of section II from 75 to 90 'to give better representation to the Social Sciences' and by electing as well five new fellows in social science and philosophy annually in addition to those to fill vacancies.[14] Thereafter there was a steady accretion of social scientists in the section – in 1941 the sociologist Carl Dawson, S.A. Cudmore of the Dominion Bureau of Statistics, the anthropologist T.F. McIlwraith from Toronto, and the historian A.R.M. Lower from Winnipeg joined – until by the late 1940s about half of the 87 members were political economists or historians who closely identified with that sprawling subject.

The decision of 1941 coincided exactly with the influx of social scientists into the expanded bureaucracy of wartime Ottawa, where they served in such bodies as External Affairs, the Wartime Prices and Trade Board, and committees on postwar reconstruction. Expansion of government activity after 1945 and reliance on civil service expertise brought to fruition the aspirations of Adam Shortt and Robert Coats. In 1956 the social sciences were put on an equal basis in a new designation: section I became 'Humanités et sciences sociales' and section II 'Humanities and Social Sciences.' The Royal Society in that year decided to establish an award for achievement in the social sciences. At first it was to be named for Innis, but at the request of section I it became the Innis-Gérin medal.

This struggle for the recognition of the social sciences within the Royal Society is significant beyond its immediate importance. It was no small part of the process affecting the character of membership at large and the steady increase in the professional status of fellows. Academics constituted about one-third of section II in 1920, half in 1940, and 85 of 104 members in 1961. By then some 37 of the academics were from the University of Toronto, a figure partially explained by that institution's dominance in the social sciences and history.

Accommodation of the social sciences revealed a tendency within the section – it had happened earlier in the sciences – to think of membership in the society as recognizing not merely individual merit and fair representation of all parts of Canada but also representation of fields. This belief was most pronounced among the social sciences, first in political economy and later in sociology and psychology, which were struggling for acceptance and status in the intellectual and university communities. That sociologists and psychologists carried away the impression that the society was not in sympathy with their subjects is understandable; indeed the society has been criticized by outside observers precisely because election of new members by existing ones reduced 'the chances of relatively young candidates, or of scholars of any age in the new fields of sociology or geography being admitted.'[15]

Finally, the relations of the social sciences to the Royal Society illuminated the mutual isolation of the French and English members. Development of the social sciences in the inter-war period was very much an English-Canadian affair, and formal connections between French and English political economists were limited: Edouard Montpetit was the only French Canadian on the executive of the Canadian Political Science Association. As is explained in the next chapter, developments within the French-language section made it not only unsympathetic to the social sciences but hostile. Léon Gérin's legacy did not live on in section I, even though he became the society's president. Jean-Charles Falardeau, who did much to revive the social sciences in Quebec after the early 1940s, recalled that he had hardly heard of Gérin during his student days at Laval and discovered his marvellous studies only later, in the library of the University of Chicago.[16]

6

French-English Relations
to Mid-Century

A salient feature of the Royal Society was that it encompassed French and English Canadians, a combination that was often commented on and embellished. In his presidential address in 1908 Samuel E. Dawson reminded his listeners that the society combined two models – the Royal Society of London, founded to increase natural knowledge, and the Académie français, for purely literary ends and maintenance of the purity of the language. The Canadian society was established 'upon the broad basis of the experience of two races, two nationalities, and two languages – a counterpart of Canada itself.' In so far as the society was concerned, Pierre Chauveau was closer to the mark when he compared Canada to the famous staircase of the Château de Chambord, which was designed so that two people could climb it without meeting except at intervals.[1] Section I gave French-Canadian fellows a solid base within the society and allowed several of them to carry on the leading roles exercised earlier by Benjamin Sulte and Marius Barbeau.

At the beginning the French Canadians whom Lorne consulted seemed content with a language section of their own even though other advisers such as Daniel Wilson thought it unfortunate that students of the same history were so divided. Like the other departments, section I was virtually autonomous; apart from participating in business affairs of the entire society, it elected its own members, planned its program independantly, and met separately. Between 1882 and 1917 the two sections devoted to history and literature had virtually no contact with each other as sections. George M. Grant in 1891 gave one reason for this: 'If we could speak French as freely and accurately as our French Canadian compatriots speak English,' he said, the two separate sections might not be necessary. 'But we cannot. Our education was neglected, and we are now too stupid to learn. I hope that it shall be otherwise with our children.' On the twenty-fifth anniversary of the society, another fellow testified that the reality of the two sections bore witness to 'the permanent co-existence of both languages' and hoped that time would 'diminish and help remove a certain nervousness on the subject which is now fading away, if not wholly departed.'[2]

The Royal Society of Canada was formally bilingual. The title page of its *Transactions* was in both languages, French-Canadian presidents such as Chauveau and Hamel gave their addresses to the whole society exclusively in French, and the papers – and poems – of section I appeared in that language. Other features of bilingualism came more slowly; it was only in 1906 and at the request of section I that the by-laws of the society were translated into French, and only in 1940 that a French-language co-editor of the *Transactions* was named. When in 1915 scientists forced a splitting of the *Transactions* so that publications of sections III and IV appeared independently, sections I and II insisted on putting out a joint volume, with essays in French and English intermingled. There were also in the council of the society and in the principle of rotation of presidents occasions for mixing together; in 1912–13, however, all members of the council except Benjamin Sulte were Anglo-Canadians. Of the 31 presidents of the society between 1882 and 1913 nine were French and 22 English (12 of whom were from the science sections). The presidency was shared not between the two language groups but among the four and later five sections. With creation of section V in 1918 the proportion of French-Canadian presidents fell; between 1920 and 1939 there were four.

The French Canadians were a minority within the society in a double sense. They constituted one-quarter of the membership initially, and over a long period, with the growth in the numbers of anglophone scientists, this proportion declined to about one-sixth by 1939. They were a minority also in that the sciences were represented by English Canadians and by British immigrants. The weakness of the French in the sciences was often remarked on, usually by French presidents, who explained this fact in terms of the preference in their culture for careers in the liberal professions of law and medicine or journalism and belles-lettres or the priesthood.

This discrepancy in the degree of support for science was naturally reflected in the membership of the Royal Society. In 1882 section IV contained two French Canadians; in 1900 only one, J.C.K. Laflamme of Laval; and in 1912, none. In section III in 1882 four fellows had French names; in 1900, three of 25; in 1912 only two, Thomas-Etienne Hamel, an ecclesiastical and educational administrator at Laval who was a teacher rather than a research scientist, and Edouard Deville, the French-born and -educated surveyor general of dominion lands. Abbé Henri Simard was elected to section III in 1923, but he, like Hamel, was more a teacher, of the physical sciences and astronomy, and popularizer, whose text in physics was widely used in the classical colleges of Quebec. In the new section V in 1920 there were three French Canadians – two priests, Victor A. Huard and Alexandre Vauchon, and Arthur Vallée. They published their papers in French, and thus that section in their eyes was bilingual.

That there were obstacles to the pursuit of science in French Quebec, a suspicion of its materialistic and irreligious implications, is evident not only in the case of

Hamel's encounter with Darwinism but also in the extent to which both Gérin and Montpetit felt it necessary to justify sociology and political economy as compatible with religious teaching and the national interest of French Canadians. Though after 1920 the outlook for the sciences was brighter, due in no small part to the efforts of the botanist and priest Marie-Victorin, the initial imbalance of the two language groups in the scientific sections persisted, with cumulative results. As late as 1951 it was pointed out that the proportion of French Canadians in the entire Canadian scientific community was only 5 per cent.[3] By that date there were 13 French Canadians, including nine in the section devoted to the biological sciences, among over 275 active members of the three science sections.

Some scientists saw the War of 1914–18 as inaugurating a new era for science; that conflict also brought to a climax a long-standing difference between French and English Canadians over the very nature of their country and its obligations to the empire. Inevitably these issues came to the forefront of attention within the Royal Society. In 1915 Louvigny T. de Montigny, a translator to the Canadian Senate, and Léon Gérin carried through section I a war resolution stating that because Canada's two mother countries were involved, because Canada was faced with the task of mobilizing thousands of volunteers in a war for freedom and humanity, and because German conduct was barbaric, the society could not stand by without voicing its indignation at the atrocities and crimes of destruction of the enemy. No other section discussed such a declaration, but the society at its general meeting resolved – on a motion of Rodolphe Lemieux, the Liberal member of the House of Commons for Gaspé and former postmaster general, and Judge James W. Longley of Nova Scotia – to 'voice our loathing of the atrocities and depredations ... committed by our foes.'[4] For good measure, Albert Lozeau added four 'Poèmes contra les Boches' praying for the deliverance of France and Alsace.

Those members of section I who commented on the issues in the war were preoccupied with two subjects. The first was the religious and philosophical meaning of the war in its broadest sense. The 76-year-old Sir Adolphe Routhier, a charter member, jurist, and prolific author (he wrote the French version of 'O Canada'), expanded on the usual wartime image of Germany as barbaric by saying that the great error of the time brought about by science and the German philosophy was to substitute a belief in humanity for a belief in God. The conflict against the German spirit was one for a Christian civilization shared by Protestants and Catholics. Clerical leaders in the section also connected the war with the old conflict of church and state, identifying Germany with a delusion that had been embraced by their liberal critics in Canada. Louis Nazaire Cardinal Bégin attested to the persistence of the ultra-montanist tradition when he attacked the misconception that the state was all, the church merely a dependant. While church and state were distinct, separation was contrary to reason and faith. The state was independent in its own sphere, but this autonomy was relative, for in the spiritual realm and in all things pertaining to the ends of the church the state was subordinate. And the theologian Mgr Louis-Adolphe Paquet reminded his listeners of the German war against the church in the Bismarck era and said that this resulted in pantheism and materialism and ultimately in the philosophy of might is right. In 1919 Lemieux, who lost a son at Arras, reiterated that man was the product not of nature but of God and the successful outcome of the war had preserved Christian civilization.[5]

The second matter was closer to home – the Canadian 'duality' and the language rights of French Canadians outside Quebec. Certain elements in section I had displayed passionate concern with the French language, not only in preserving its purity (as Lorne had expected them to do) but with its status as an indication of the equality of the two linguistic groups in Canada as a whole. Adjutor Rivard, a lawyer and founder of the Société du Parler français du Canada in 1902, marked its tenth anniversary in 1912, the year he was president of section I, with the first Congrés de la Langue française in Quebec City. At this assembly delegates from Ontario, Acadia, and the west, as well as Quebec, resolved to defend French-language rights against Regulation 17, which had curtailed use of French in the schools of Ontario.

This controversy extended into the war years. Routhier pleaded for other provinces to respect the rights of French-speaking peoples to have their children educated in French, just as the same rights of the English minority were respected in Quebec. The archbishop of Montreal, Paul Bruchési, devoted a lecture to outlining both the constitutional basis and the historical practice of accepting the equality of the two languages – a legal and moral right that temporary majorities should not affect. In 1916 the society, on a motion of Bruchési and Principal Peterson of McGill, implored schools in the English parts of Canada to pay more attention to study of the French language and literature.[6]

Such well-intentioned resolutions could not arrest the developing rupture over conscription in 1917, with its supporters claiming that it was essential for preserving Canada's commitment in a war against barbarism and for sustaining Canada's claim for an autonomous status within the empire, and its critics (most but not all of whom were French Canadians) maintaining that Canadians should not be coerced into fighting British wars. After introduction of conscription and the isolation of Quebec in the election of 1917 French Canada turned inward and accentuated its nationalism and social conservatism. Both tendencies were reflected directly within the Royal Society. On one level, section I had been defined in terms of certain subjects studied in the French language; increasingly, however, it became clear that section I constituted an ethnic identity and was seen to represent French Canada within the society, just as Quebec was regarded as the homeland of French Canada within the Confederation. In 1918 Marius Barbeau urged that the transactions for section I contain the papers of those members of the scientific sections who published in French – a proposal turned down by the society then and later. In 1921 section I rejected the notion – to which the rest of the society paid lip service – that members had to attend and contribute papers at least once every three years and decided to hold separate meetings of the section in Quebec, Montreal, and Ottawa in order to make the purposes of the society better known. In 1924 the botanist frère Marie-Victorin was elected to section I, even though his disciplinary association seemed more appropriate for section V, on the biological sciences (to which in fact he was transferred in 1927).[7] Victorin himself suggested that section I consider creating a French-language scientific section.

The tendency to identify section I with an ethnic group as well as areas of scholarly activity was evident in the case of Harry Ashton, who taught French literature at the University of British Columbia and was elected a member of section II in 1923. Ashton's papers on Diderot and on the study of French literature in Canadian universities were delivered to, and published by, the English literary section. Many years later H.F. Angus, a colleague of Ashton's, commented on this odd situation: 'To a man whose published work was mainly in French and whose field of scholarship was French, it was incomprehensible that recognition in a *soi-disant* bilingual country should not have come from the French-speaking Section. A frank explanation was rather humiliating for a Canadian to give and perhaps today the attitude of Section I is less exclusive.'[8]

This tendency to equate section I with French-Canadian ethnicity was paralleled after 1920 by increasing emphasis on traditional nationalism and social conservatism. This situation was, of course, not entirely novel, for before the war the history of French Canada had been assiduously cultivated, its language studied and defended, and social commentary was critical of early claims for wider female rights or government intervention to improve the state of the working class.[9] But before the war there seemed a more complex ideological mix in section I, where the liberal tradition of French Canada, with its opposition to clerical intervention in politics, was represented by Benjamin Sulte and others, and where the social sciences had made such promising beginnings with Gérin and Bouchette.

In the inter-war years the papers published by section I read like an anthology of a nationalism that highlighted historical memory, faith, language, and survival. A marked increase in the number of priests in the section led to growth in the number of their publications. In 1921 there were 34 members in the section, nine of them priests, an increase from four in 1908. In 1935 of 39 fellows, 11 were clergymen. In 1939 of 13 papers printed by that section, eight were written by priests.[10] (In section II in 1921 only four were identified as clergymen, and none was elected as such after 1906.)

Among the frequent clerical contributors was the theologian and author of multi-volume commentaries in Latin on St Thomas, L.-A. Paquet, who in 1928 pronounced that rationalism and positivism were incapable of rising to the summits of either history or science, a point made earlier by abbé Arthur Robert in an extended discussion of Comte and Durkheim, morality and sociology, emphasizing the need to subordinate the material to the spiritual. In 1934 Paquet took the anniversary of Jacques Cartier's voyage and his planting of the cross as an opportunity to confirm that from its birth French Canada had been guided, indeed dominated, by a religious mission. Mgr Médard Emard, archbishop of Ottawa, had in 1926 celebrated the beatification the previous year of the Jesuit Martyrs of Huronia, who he claimed had imprinted on a whole people an apostolic mission. E.-J. Auclair, archbishop of Montreal in 1936, when the issue of enfranchising Quebec women in provincial elections was being debated, reminded females of their 'mission providentielle.' 'Notre femme d'habitant,' he declared ' ... forte et active au travail, est encore et toujours, après quelques années de convent, une gardienne irréductible de nos traditions catholiques, de nos coutumes ancestrales, de nôtre langue, même si elle ne la parle pas aussi correctement qu'elle pourait le faire, et par suite de nôtre survivance français.'[11]

The sense of religious mission, the primacy of the ideal, and the elevation of changelessness into a cardinal virtue were most extensively articulated in a ten-article series on the life of the spirit in French Canada by Mgr Emile Chartier of the Université de Montréal. Published between 1930 and 1939 and an able survey of the arts, letters, journalism, history, eloquence, and poetry, Chartier's series dwelt on the theme of preserving and reproducing all that had been brought from pre-revolutionary France. 'La conservation intégrale de la parler atteste la préoccupation essentielle du peuple canadien-français: garder sans altération de caractère reçu des ancêstres.' In explaining the role of history as a stimulant to national consciousness Chartier said that French Canada stood in the same relation to materialistic North America as old France did to Europe: 'Le gardien des traditions de foi, de justice et d'honneur, le porte drapeau de l'idéalisme intellectuel et moral.'[12]

The contributions of historians in the 1920s and 1930s, while not necessarily so expansive in generalizing, were entirely compatible with these views. Ivanhoë Caron, who gave up labours as a parish priest to work in the Bureau des archives du Québec, published some 17 essays and scrupulously edited documents, among them a history of the parish of Saint-Ignace de Cap Saint-Ignace, filled with lovingly recovered details of settlers, seigneurs, the first church, and parish priests. Gustave Lanctot of the Public Archives in Ottawa published a good deal in the 1930s on the themes of the 'prodigieux miracle' of survival, the relations of French and English, and the recent influences of the United States on French Canada, a subject on which he was supposed to do a study for the Carnegie Series. 'Americanism,' which he identified with sensationalism, agnosticism, 'le gangstérisme' of the movies, and divorce, had made no inroads on the mentality of the people of Quebec. They preferred moral satisfaction and contentment over riches and remained faithful to the idealism, individualism, and traditionalism that sustained their ethnic identity.[13] On another plane, studies appearing in the *Transactions* for section I on folkways and the craftsmanship of silversmiths, and reports on government efforts to support and revivify the art of wood carving, fitted the same mould.

The tenets of traditional nationalism would in time come to be regarded as grotesque oversimplifications and impediments to Quebec's and Canada's development. It should be emphasized, therefore, that those in the interwar years who upheld these convictions were members of the Royal Society, a pan-Canadian institution, and they saw themselves as working toward better understanding between French and English Canadians. Emile Chartier in 1928 took note of the idea espoused by some in the Action canadienne-française of an independent French and Catholic state on the St Lawrence and rejected this separatism on the grounds that the survival of French Canada depended on the strength of numbers of francophones not only in Quebec but in all of Canada.[14] (The many papers on the Métis of the west by Judge Prud'homme in these decades helped sustain the view of a Canada-wide French presence.)

Perhaps the best example of the *bonne entente* tradition in this period was the priest Camille Roy, who taught at Laval and wrote extensively on French-Canadian literature, which he saw as a repository of the spirit of the people. He was in effect the soul mate of Lorne Pierce, editor of the Ryerson Press and literary nationalist, who dedicated his outline history of Canadian literature to Roy, and who must have been especially pleased when in 1929 Roy was awarded the medal he had endowed. In 1929 Roy took as the subject of his presidential address 'Provincialisme intellectuel au Canada'; by this he meant 'deux cultures,' one rooted in French Quebec, the other patterned after Ontario, each with distinct characteristics, ways of thinking and understanding. As conveyed in literature, the Latin spirit excelled in literary culture, theological speculation, and abstract principles; the English were more oriented to the sciences and their practical application and to economic life. Roy celebrated this dualism as enriching and saw it embodied in the Royal Society no less than in Confederation. And he emphasized his belief that the *bonne entente* and cooperation would ensure moral unity and solidarity. Like Pierce and other English-Canadian literary nationalists in the 1920s Roy too lamented the fact that Canadians were spending $15 million a year on American publications, which inhibited growth of the national spirit in the country.[15] That French and English were endowed with complementary characteristics was an old idea, and one that found its resonance in political relations of the two groups. For almost a century after Confederation the French were content to leave the material development of the country to the English, so long as they could preserve their culture.

The relations of French and English in the larger world found other parallels within the Royal Society. One of the striking features of French-Canadian leadership in the society was the crucial place of employees of the dominion government and, to a lesser extent, academics from Laval. Civil servants, of course, were numerous in all the sections but the French language group was an exaggerated case. Mention has been made of Benjamin Sulte, who was for forty years ubiquitous in the society's affairs, and of Marius Barbeau, who was equally prominent in the interwar period and treasurer of the society 1920–6 (the only French Canadian to hold that position till the 1980s). Arthur Beauchesne, clerk of the Commons, was, like his predecessor Bourinot, both an authority on parliamentary procedure and secretary of the society 1936–40; Gustave Lanctot, a veteran of the Great War and dominion archivist 1937–48, was prominent in the society's activities, as were two of his employees – François-Joseph Audet, head of the information bureau from 1906 to 1943, and Séraphin Marion, director of publications from 1925 to 1954. Marion in 1940 became the first francophone secretary of the society and was succeeded by Pierre Daviault, a close student of the evolution of the two languages and supervisor of the translation bureau of the House of Commons.

This group was so prominent within section I and in representing it within the society partly because section I was relatively small, despite formal equality of allotted membership with section II. For some reason section I did not elect the numbers to which it was entitled. The resulting divergence became evident after the Great War: in 1922 section I had 37 fellows and section II, 49. By 1942 the figures were, respectively, 36 and 77, and in 1962, 82 and 155.[16] Naturally the size of section I affected numbers attending annual sessions. Meetings in Ottawa, Montreal, and Quebec City drew more than other places, but even the national capital in 1936 attracted only 13, five of whom (mentioned above) lived there. (Numbers for other sections that year were II, 43; III, 44; IV, 43; and V, 38.) Toronto had always seemed especially uninviting: in meetings there section I was represented by four in 1902, nine in 1931, and ten in 1946. As the society ventured further afield attendance did not increase: 11 members of section I went to Winnipeg in 1928, eight to London in 1940, 11 to Hamilton in 1943, seven to Kingston in 1945, and 13 to Halifax in 1949. Such figures makes one wonder about the Royal Society as a forum for exchange of viewpoints, not only between the language groups but within section I itself.

The dependence of section I on the mediations of a relatively small group was extended beyond the Second World War. In the 1950s the bedrock of the French group consisted of Louis-Philippe Audet, son of François, and a historian of Quebec's educational system; Jean Bruchési, Quebec civil servant and historian who in 1959 became Canada's ambassador to Spain; Jean-Charles Bonenfant, once secretary to Premier Duplessis and from 1939 librarian of the Quebec legislature; and Guy Sylvestre, who worked in the Library of Parliament, was private secretary to Prime Minister Louis St Laurent 1945–50, and in 1968 became national librarian. Université Laval provided the historian abbé Arthur Maheux, who shared the outlook of Camille Roy, and Maurice Lebel, who, according to his own calculations, published 21 articles in the *Transactions* between 1943 and 1978, more than anyone else in section I in that period.[17] Among the small minority of French-Canadian scientists prominent in the society's business were Léo Marion, a native of Ottawa and a chemist who served on the editorial staff of the NRC publications, and Léon Lortie, who taught chemistry at Montréal and, like Marie-Victorin earlier, was an energetic popularizer of science. Sylvestre, Bruchési, Daviault, Lebel, Léo Marion, Lortie, and Lanctot would be presidents of the Royal Society in the two decades after the Second World War.

These French Canadians at the centre of the society were in some respects atypical of French-Canadian intellectual leaders. Their employment in Ottawa brought them into daily contact with English Canadians, and their understanding of the relations of the two linguistic communities was no doubt informed by these experiences. Professionally they occupied a curious niche at the point of political contact between French and English Canada. Their educations were in some cases unusual too: Barbeau had been a Rhodes scholar, Léo Marion had attended Queen's and McGill, and Lortie had studied at Paris and Cornell. Lanctot, who had studied at Oxford, served in the war in an English-speaking unit. They tended to involve themselves in organizations that were national in purpose and membership. At times Barbeau seemed to be everywhere, in the Canadian Historical Association in its early years and on the editorial board of the *Canadian Geographic Journal*. (He would resign from the Royal Society in 1947 because it could not publish all his papers and those of promising scholars that he brought to it.) Séraphin Marion, who had taught French briefly at the Royal Military College at Kingston, had in the late 1920s lectured across the country under the auspices of the Association of Canadian Clubs on French-English cooperation. Lanctot, Maheux, and Marion had close contacts with the small community of English-Canadian historians: in the 20 years after 1934 Lanctot, F.-J. Audet, Maheux, and Bruchési were presidents of the Canadian Historical Association.

Ottawa gave these people a unique point of view on French Canada. Like Gérin they were French-Canadian patriots, yet, equally, they were critical of certain features of French Quebec, of its neglect of the sciences, or of the excesses of its nationalism. It should be recalled that it was Arthur Beauchesne who urged dissolution of section I and its recombination into a literature group that would include English-Canadian literary scholars and writers. Beauchesne in 1938 could be acerbic in describing the literary consequences of French-Canadian isolation. 'For over a century,' he wrote, 'we had no other secondary education than a few seminaries whose teachers were more virtuous than competent. They either had no libraries or very limited ones in which masterpieces were excluded if they were not ultramontane, jansenistic, or intensely religious. There is still a school in Quebec which claims that what is on the *Index Expurgatoris* is not literature.'[18]

As a group, these men disapproved of another tradition within French Canada that was an outgrowth of conservative nationalism and whose major interpreter was abbé Lionel Groulx. Groulx began to teach Canadian history at Montreal in 1915, and his views quickly came to the notice of the Royal Society. At the 1916 meeting a young lawyer, Antonio Perrault, had a paper read on Montalembert's opinions of Canada, and in it he cited Groulx's lectures. Montalembert was wrong, said Perrault, to praise the British regime for recognizing and preserving French Canada's rights; its religion, laws, and language had been maintained not by British magnanimity but by constant struggle, sometimes against Tories, to whom Perrault referred as 'les Allemands' of their times. At no point in their experience, in 1760, 1837, or 1916, were the French permitted a false sense of security, for the keynote of their history was one of resolute defence of their Catholic and French character against ever-present attempts at assimilation if not humiliation. Perrault caught the essentials of Groulx's message. Groulx would go on to describe Confederation as a compact, broken many times by Anglo-Canadians, and celebrate an idealized New France, the source of ancestral virtues.

Groulx was elected to the Royal Society in 1918, an unsought honour according to his memoirs and a difficult occasion because before the voting Duncan Campbell Scott had sent out to members examples of some suspect passages in his lectures. Groulx's supporters, however, stuck to their guns and saved the autonomy of section I.[19] Groulx attended the Winnipeg meeting in 1928 but virtually no others; he sent in an abstract in 1935, 'La Jeuness démocratique de 1848,' but published no papers in the *Transactions*. His view of Canadian history did not go unchallenged: during the Second World War abbé Maheux criticized Groulx for propagating an interpretation of the past that exaggerated malice, as opposed to ignorance, in misunderstandings and helped keep Canadians apart. In 1945 Groulx, Barbeau, the novelist Philippe Panneton (whose pen name was Ringuet), the historians Robert Rumilly and Guy Frégault, and others launched the Académie canadienne-française. It was, in the words of Mason Wade, 'a revolt against the artificial yoking of two distinct colonial cultures in the Royal Society of Canada, whose French-Canadian elder statesmen no longer commanded much respect from the younger generation in Quebec. Many of the members of the new Academy were nationalists who held that French- and English-Canadian cultures were irreconcilable, and that the Royal Society was merely a mutual admiration society of bonne-ententistes.'[20] None the less, Groulx accepted the Tyrrell medal in 1948 – the citation read: 'Le Chanoine Groulx croit à l'impartialité au histoire, mais non à l'impassibilité'[21] – and resigned from the society in 1952.

Groulx started an institute at the Université de Montréal in 1946 for the study of French America and the *Revue d'histoire de l'Amérique française* the next year. Three young historians, Michel Brunet, Guy Frégault, and Maurice Séguin, who would reorient French-Canadian historical writing in the following decades, drew their inspiration partly from Groulx. None of them became a member of the Royal Society.[22]

7

Postwar Malaise

As early as 1939 it seemed to thoughtful observers within the society that its parts had become more important than the whole. The sections had developed distinct personalities, and as an institution the society appeared to be a congeries of interest groups, if not independent estates. This fragmentation was visible in the *Transactions*, published in separate parts for each of the scientific sections, and it was frequently deplored in presidential addresses devoted to clarifying the society's objectives. In 1938 the marine biologist A.G. Huntsman found an appropriate analogy in comparing the society to 'the common five-finger or starfish of our Atlantic coast, which, if placed on its back, takes a long time to right itself, since each of the five arms for a time at least gives expression to only its own idea of what should be done under the circumstances. Our five Sections ... not only slow down any necessary corporate action, but, when acting very effectively as units, tend to make us lose sight of what we might accomplish as a body.' Huntsman thought that the society was failing – not really bringing together diverse experiences and knowledge in genuine interchanges.[1] In 1940, as we saw above, H.M. Tory came to much the same conclusion, decrying the chasm between the sciences and humanities and judging that the units of the society were cooperating in form but not in substance.

No action to counteract centrifugal tendencies was taken during the war of 1939–45, and in the two decades following the making of peace the Canadian environment proved favourable to the society and at the same time intensified its problems. Canadians emerged from the war filled with a spirit of self-confidence and a sense that the country had come of age; some of the last residues of colonialism ended with creation of separate Canadian citizenship and termination of appeals to the Judicial Committee of the Privy Council. This feeling of optimism was buoyed up by unprecedented economic prosperity, satisfaction with the beginnings of the welfare state, and ready acceptance of international responsibilities in the new Commonwealth, the United Nations, and the North Atlantic Treaty Organization. The hopefulness about Canada's prospects in some ways revived the aspirations of cultural nationalists of the 1920s for literary and artistic maturity.

Reports on the state of the humanities and social sciences, however, were suffused with gloom, especially regarding lack of financial support and departure of so many highly educated Canadians to the United States. In the postwar years the Royal Society revived its scholarship program with funds from some provinces, augmented by the Carnegie Corporation, and, after 1953, it was jointly responsible for selecting winners of the Canadian Government Overseas Awards made possible by use of currency balances owed to Canada by European countries. (As before, some of those helped would become illustrious in their fields – Earle Birney, Anne Hébert, and George Woodcock in literature, Alfred Pellan and Goodrich Roberts in art, Charles Taylor in philosophy, Louis Siminovitch in medicine, Fernand Dumont in sociology, and Marcel Trudel in history.) In 1954–5 the society granted 27 scholarships and fellowships for which there were 364 applicants. In a report on scholarship in Canada commissioned by the Canadian Social Science Research Council in 1945 the expatriate Canadian historian at Columbia University, John Bartlet Brebner, confirmed that it lacked adequate support and incidentally depicted the Royal Society as ineffectual and of slight influence, saying that its 'meetings have been rather drowsy gatherings of pleasant urbanity, but little distinction, and the transactions slumber for the most part undisturbed on library shelves.'

The most vigorous scholarly work was being done elsewhere, in the specialized journals and associations, at the NRC and the universities; for Brebner the letters 'FRSC' gave 'off an honorific, autumnal glow which is comfortable rather than stimulating.' (Brebner refrained from mentioning the increasing prominence of lengthy obituaries in the *Transactions* after the mid-1930s.) For this detached observer, not known for erratic judgments, the Royal Society's membership was too large, too old, and virtually irrelevant.[2]

Yet better times lay ahead, signalized by appointment in 1949 of the Royal Commission on National Development in the Arts, Letters and Sciences chaired by Vincent Massey. The Massey Commission paid far more attention to the humanities than to the sciences, presumably because the latter already enjoyed considerable state support, and its mandate included broadcasting policy and university financing. In August 1949, the Royal Society made one of the 473 representations received by the commission, a memorial that seemed concerned more with advancing its own interests than with cultural policy in general. It endorsed a more comprehensive program of university scholarships and post-doctoral fellowships in the humanities to be administered by the society and requested an endowment fund sufficient to produce $30,000 a year as well as adequate headquarters. It urged that the state make a practice of appointing members of the Royal Society as such to all boards and commissions dealing with science or humane learning, and to government delegations to international functions having to do with these subjects, and that the government recognize the society as its 'permanent advisor' in matters relating to research and advancement of knowledge. It also supported building of a National Library, National Gallery, Botanical Garden, and a new Museum of Archaeology, Ethnology and Natural Science.[3]

These latter projects were endorsed by many other institutions and groups; the society's case for a National Library, for example, was made in conjunction with the Canadian Historical Association, the Canadian Library Association, the Canadian Political Science Association, and the Social Science Research Council. The founding of the Canada Council in 1957 relieved the society of the task of administering its own Canada Research Fellowships; it also marked the beginning of a 'change of the intellectual climate in Canada' and an upsurge of research and publication in the humanities and social sciences. At a later date the society would contrast the state of things in 1947 and 1964: 'We move from an atmosphere of gloom and stoical resolution to one of buoyancy and expectation.'[4] The society in this period became dependent on the Canada Council just as it had earlier relied on the NRC. In 1969 it received $17,000 from the NRC, $10,000 from the Canada Council, and $2,500 from provincial governments. (It also raised $9,750 from fees, $8,500 from sales of its publications, and $7,500 interest on its investments in municipal bonds.)[5]

The society became more outward looking in the postwar years and extended the geographic range of its meeting places. In 1942 about two-thirds of its fellows came from Toronto (83), Ottawa (62), and Montreal (61), and the society naturally tended to meet in those three cities, with occasional ventures to Quebec City, Halifax, Kingston, and London. In 1948 it reached the campus of the University of British Columbia. 'Our Western members,' it was reported, 'are beginning to resent very much the expense to which they are put in continually making the long journey to Eastern centres.'⁶ In the following years, the society convened in Winnipeg (1954), Saskatoon (1959), Charlottetown (1964), Calgary (1968), and St John's (1972), in addition to Ottawa and other familiar haunts. The BC meeting in 1948 was held at the same time as the sessions of the Canadian Historical Association, the Canadian Humanities Research Council, the Canadian Institute of International Affairs, and the Canadian Social Science Research Council. About 1960 some 26 other societies met in the two-week period around the date of the Royal Society's sessions in June and in the same centre. (The society met every second year in Ottawa; in 1967 it moved from the NRC to the new National Library.) While these contemporaneous meetings may attest to its continuing maternal role in maintaining contact with some of its offspring, this link was necessary for the society's own welfare, for only if there were sufficient numbers of specialists from these other organizations in attendance would the society receive papers of high calibre. In 1950 the society named chairs of regional centres and dispatched speakers – W.H. Alexander, Lebel, and Sandwell – to address them.

In the mid-1950s, the society launched two series in an effort to reach a wider audience than the *Transactions* enjoyed. The first series, Special Publications (see Appendix, part A), consisted of scientific papers on a single theme, such as soils in Canada, or continental drift. Suitably enough, one of the early volumes was a collection of the publications of William F. Ganong on crucial maps and place nomenclature of the Atlantic coast of Canada. The second series, Studia Varia (Appendix, part B), by 1970 was made up of 14 short books of essays from interdisciplinary symposia. These series mark both the beginning of a substantial publication program on the part of the society, which had previously concentrated on the *Transactions*, and growing uneasiness over hyper-specialization and an effort to cross boundaries. Increasingly in the postwar years papers that reported the details of research were supplanted by more general appraisals of trends and tendencies in Canada and the world and by explorations of subjects that lent themselves to analysis from more than one disciplinary standpoint.

The idea of 'symposia' goes back at least to H.M. Tory's suggestion in 1940 of topics that would bring scientists and humanists closer together. In 1942 there was a joint session of all sections on postwar reconstruction, with geologists in particular demonstrating enthusiasm for planned use of resources, and in 1946 section II held a symposium on traditional disciplines and the history of ideas, with papers in history, literature, and philosophy. Intellectual history at this time seemed to offer one way of reintegrating areas of study that had become separated.

There was an additional consideration that made symposia attractive. In the 1940s and 1950s the intellectual elites in the United States and Britain turned their attention to defence of the beliefs and values that the Western democracies were defending first against Nazism and then against Stalinist totalitarianism. The Massey Commission had said that cultural defences as well as military strength had to be made secure. The liberal tradition of the West consisted of individual freedoms and democracy, and it was embodied in the fine arts, the literature of Greece and Rome, and the reflections of the best minds of the ages. Mobilization of intellectual resources in the Cold War left a deep imprint on humanists in the Royal Society.

'A terrible menace now hangs over the world,' declared Jean Bruchési in 1951, 'and this menace which threatens occidental civilization, and hence Christian culture, does not come from the exterior only, but also from within. We are justly concerned not only with the danger of a deadly conflict between two powerful forces, but with the consequences of such a conflict for our civilization. The weapons of war, however perfect they are, cannot alone protect us from this danger ... One cannot defend what one does not believe in, ... But one fights for one's life, for one's property, for one's soul; so one is ready to fight for one's moral and intellectual values.'[7] Concern with 'moral and intellectual values' suffused symposia in section II in the 1950s: one in 1951 was entitled 'Guides and Philosophers in an Age of Anxiety' and included a lecture by Frank Underhill on Arnold J. Toynbee, the philosopher-historian who had traced the rise and fall of civilization in search for the reasons for their vitality and decline, and another on Reinhold Neibuhr, the American theologian whose teachings centred on the reality of human evil. With the explosions over Hiroshima and Nagasaki a very fresh memory in 1952 section II held a joint session with section III on 'Man and the World in an Age of Science.' The renewed determination to preserve a heritage rejuvenated classical studies; in 1951 W.H. Alexander gave a lecture, 'The Religion of Classicism,' to the 11 regional centres of the society, including Quebec City and Montreal, where he spoke in French. Maurice Lebel was no less energetic in linking the classics to contemporary requirements, offering an illustration of how anxieties generated by the Cold War tended to unite French- and English-Canadian intellectuals.

This greater respect for ideas and beliefs was expressed by the shift in historical writing from preoccupation with economic history and the economic interpretation of history in the 1930s to political biography in the 1950s, a development that was to accentuate a growing rift between history and the social sciences. Donald G. Creighton led the way in this direction both with his biography of Sir John A. Macdonald and with his defence of the autonomy of historical thinking as distinct from social science. However, he gave little to the society to which he was elected in 1946 and which in 1951 awarded him –

and Jean Bruchési – Tyrrell medals. (This was the first time two such medals were given in one year, and the *Transactions* reported his name as D.A. Creighton.)

These attitudes went hand in hand with pronounced disdain for contemporary 'mass culture' of the radio, news-stands, movie screens, and advertising, which were dismissed as levelling, mediocre, and tasteless. The Massey Commission had defended a traditional elite culture against mass entertainment emanating from the United States, and many members of the Royal Society shared this attitude, including the historian Arthur Lower, who in 1953 referred to 'the great democratic public that storms against "culture-vultures" who like to have symphonic concerts on Sunday afternoons. This great public, coming up from below, its head full of sad American slave music and its belly full of Coca-Cola, has little respect for the academic "culture"'[8] One symposium in section II in the mid-1950s centred on Hilda Neatby's *So Little for the Mind* (1954), a slashing attack on 'progressive' education, which in the name of social adjustment and democratic access had allegedly destroyed standards, literacy, and much else. Underhill correctly saw Neatby's book as another indication of the rise of conservatism in North America.

Compared to the political reticence of the society in the 1930s the members of sections I and II now became far more engaged with contemporary issues, and in this they resembled their predecessors during the First World War. None went farther than Watson Kirkconnell in denouncing the Soviet conspiracy and its Canadian accomplices, but many subjects that caught their attention were of current importance and international in range: the changing Commonwealth, the economic and political significance to Canada of NATO, Canadian aid to 'the underdeveloped world,' the UN Declaration on Human Rights and the Canadian constitution, Sputnik and the doubts this Soviet satellite raised about North American science education, and the threat of nuclear war. They worried also about technology – an apprehension that would grow, especially in the 1970s. Symposia on 'The Function of the Humanities in an Age of Technology,' (1969) and 'The Survival of Essential Human Values' (1971) would be followed by many reflections on automation, computers, the mass media, and nuclear reactors.

The scientific sections embraced the idea of symposia in the same period and concentrated on the oceans and the Arctic. In 1949 a session involving Huntsman, geophysicist Tuzo Wilson, economist D.C. MacGregor, and others focused on oceans, and by the early 1950s the papers of the Canadian Committee on Oceanography almost comprised another sectional report in the *Transactions*. Intensified interest in the Arctic was a direct byproduct of the resource boom and, above all, the fact that Canada's northern reaches had become a line of defence against the Soviet Union. The Arctic Institute of North America was founded in Montreal in 1945, and the Royal Canadian Air Force began to photograph thousands of square miles of the unmapped domain. In 1950 the Royal Society held a symposium on the far north and scientific research; the next year, thanks to the initiative of climatologist Kenneth Hare, it heard appraisals of the Arctic environment as well as reports on the northern settlement and development of the Soviet Union. The north and the oceans were brought together in a 1954 symposium sponsored by the Canadian Committee on Oceanography on the climate, patterns of ice distribution, hydrography, and biology of Hudson Bay.

In the two decades after the war the north assumed a dominant place in the deliberations of the Royal Society. This fascination was expressed in technical studies of permafrost and geological structure and, by the 1960s, estimates of energy resources and environmental deterioration. The north appealed to the historian W.L. Morton, who traced its influence on Canadian experience, and the literary critic Desmond Pacey, who examined the images of the climate of Canada in fiction and poetry and found that 'the great majority ... relate to ice, snow and frost.' In 1950 Hugh Keenleyside, deputy minister of resources and development, sent a paper to the first symposium on the Arctic that sounded the note of an ancient element of Canadian mythology. Canada's north, he asserted, 'nourished social and political democracy, independence and self-reliance, freedom in cooperation, hospitality and social responsibility – all virtues of particular importance in national life.' The Canadian frontier, unlike the American one which ended around 1890, 'will be a permanent source of energy from which Canada will draw strength in the never-ending fight to guard and maintain the personal decencies and human rights of her people. As long as the frontier remains there will be Canadians who will never succumb to the designs of the totalitarian or the power of domestic tyranny. The frontier is a bastion of freedom, and the North is a permanent frontier.' Seven years later John Diefenbaker introduced his vision of the north to national politics.[9]

Symposia found favour in the science sections for additional reasons. By the early 1950s the *Transactions* no longer served as a medium for communicating scientific research. To the *Canadian Journal of Research* which had been published by the NRC since 1929 were by now added journals for chemistry, technology, physics, and mathematics. By 1951 there were some 25 scientific periodicals 'worthy of the name' published in Canada,[10] and their effects on the Royal Society's journal were severe. In 1949 there were 40 communications to section V, but only four were printed. Of 106 papers to section III, three appeared in 26 pages. In 1955 there were 119 papers on the program for section III, 90 were presented at 12 subsectional meetings, but only nine – all in mathematics – were printed in the society's journal. Scientific reportage in the *Transactions* was now essentially by brief abstracts, an indication of work being carried on rather than substantial accounts of results. (Some of the science reports of course were published more fully after 1956 in Special Publications and after 1970 in a new series, Proceedings of Symposia, also itemized in the Appendix, part C.)

It is not surprising therefore that recurrent dissatisfaction with the society and its *Transactions* should resurface at this time and that it should come initially from section III. In a 1949 report (written in part by E.W.R. Steacie, who would soon become president of the NRC) advocating reorganization of the society the physical scientists declared that 'the Royal Society is not of great value' and listed as its main defects divergence of interests between the sciences and the humanities; lack of continuity of policy and action owing to the one-year term of presidents and rotation of that office among the sections; almost total lack of activity between annual meetings; a set of highly cumbersome by-laws, which required reference back and forth among the sections; the custom of electing officers of the society and the sections as an honour rather than for their leadership capacity; and poor distribution of members among the sections. The number of fellows in a section had, they said, little or no relation to the number or quality of workers in respective fields. Section III recommended complete reorganization and splitting of the society into two branches – humanities and sciences – which, while meeting at the same time, would 'have virtually nothing to do with each other.' The presidency was to be abolished or made purely honorary. As for the science branch its president would be elected for a five-year term.[11]

These shortcomings were reinforced – and others noticed – in the next few years by other scientists. Gerhard Herzberg of the NRC pointed out in 1952 that while sections I and II had set limits to membership, the scientific sections did not, though the numbers elected in any single year were restricted, and there was a danger that one section would grow out of proportion to the others. Referring to a matter that had long irritated members of section III, he surveyed the Canadian professoriate in the subjects represented in sections III and IV and found four times as many individuals in fields represented in the former as in the latter.[12] (The total membership of the society at that time was 432, with 103 in section III and 81 in IV). A geologist would later reply by estimating that there were some 5,000 geologists in Canada, 1,280 members of the Alberta Society of Petroleum Engineers alone.[13] Section V also complained that it could in 1955 elect no more than six of 60 qualified candidates and observed that biologists were much more numerous than humanists, unlike the situation in 1882. As for the *Transactions*, it was the general impression in the society that while sections I and II were satisfied, or had mild criticisms, the opinions of the science sections were more caustic, ranging from seeing it as useless to tepid support or tolerance. The crux of the issue was still its limited circulation and appearance only once a year, which delayed publication of scientific papers.[14]

The reform agenda set out by section III in 1949 would be effected in substance, but not in all particulars, over time. The tempo of change in the Royal Society had always been measured in decades or even generations rather than years, and in this case the process was tortuous and prolonged, even by the society's standards. The three science sections were amalgamated into a single Academy of Science (academy III) in 1961 in order to 'speak with authority on behalf of science as a whole'[15] and in 1975 section I became the Académie des lettres et des sciences humaines (academy I), and section II, the Academy of Humanities and Social Sciences (academy II.) For the latter this seemed to involve little more than a change in designation; in a few years, however, it became clear that the concept of an academy implied claims for status and function that had not been a dominant feature of the society before.

These modest reforms inaugurated three decades of intense introspection into the state of the institution and its future. While stock-taking had always been a regular feature of president's addresses at both the society and sectional levels, these became more preoccupied with problems and unresolved difficulties. Some sought a sense of direction in the past, and the speeches of Lorne and Dawson in the early 1880s were intensely scrutinized. There was a widespread sense of malaise after 1960, a feeling that the society had fulfilled its original objectives and/or had been overtaken by time, that it ought to have a new role but there was little consensus on what that was to be. Committees on reorganization became permanent features of the society in these years.

In 1963 Frank Scott, poet and constitutional expert, offered an incisive and witty appraisal of the society and its mandate and concluded that little would change if it disappeared. It was dominated by older scholars, and the most original studies in all fields went elsewhere. 'The laudable purpose of bringing together literary and scientific men from both English- and French-speaking Canada is equally well if not better fulfilled in the other societies,' said this critic; 'the great difficulty in our society has been the hiving off of most of the French-speaking members in a single French-speaking section, even though the topics they discuss are the same as those being treated in Section II.' The Royal Society was struggling to adapt to a situation far different from that which existed at its birth – 'like Canada, it is searching for its own identity' – but Scott saw a glimmer of hope in its mission of working against the 'isolation of specialization.' Its other business – awarding medals and scholarships – was peripheral to this central task. 'There is always the possibility that we might grow more and more into a kind of wheel-chair

rest home, where extinct intellectual volcanoes read innu-
merable papers at each other on totally unrelated topics,
and an ever lengthening file of dull green volumes gather
dust on their widening shelves.'[16] Scott's hope for interdisciplinary communication was not universally shared.
In 1965 the society canvassed opinions on its activities
and found that most members ranked recognition of distinction first, communicating among disciplines second,
and surveys of the state of various fields third.[17]

A few years later Claude Dolman, a microbiologist at
the University of British Columbia, expressed scepticism
about concentrating on symposia and popularizing science. For him, the problem of the society was that it was
too large and too many members were apathetic. Since
1882 its membership had multiplied nine-fold while the
country's population had increased by five times. Dolman
rejected the idea that the numbers of people in disciplines
and professions in Canada at large should be reflected
exactly in the makeup of the society. In addressing specific reforms then before the body, he argued for longer
terms for officials and a strengthened secretariat, which
would provide corporate self-confidence, continuity, and a
sense of direction; supported establishment of more extensive international relations with academies abroad; and
upheld the traditional view that since the society 'offers
uniquely detached, versatile, and expert judgment in many
fields' it ought to be consulted by governments. He cast
an envious glance at Sweden's Royal Academy of Sciences, which operated several research institutes and had
a budget ten times that of the Royal Society.[18]

By the early 1970s the reform program of some scientists had crystallized around three general objectives. The
first was that the society should take the lead in drawing
matters of importance to public attention by holding symposia on a continuous basis. Such topics as mercury in the
environment, communications into the home, and energy
use were regarded as especially promising. In this con-

nection it was felt that the society should commission and direct studies and make their results available to governments. The second aim was more vigorous assertion of an international role for the society in representing Canada in such organizations as the International Council of Scientific Unions and in closer relations with other national academies. For a very long time the Royal Society had been represented at international scientific congresses and anniversaries, mainly by individual members who happened to be attending under other auspices or simply visiting the countries where these events took place. The society had in 1909 been represented at the celebration in Cambridge, England, of the half-century of Darwin's *Origin of Species*, and H.M. Tory and the geologist Frank Adams were its delegates to the Pan Pacific Science Congress in Tokyo in 1926. In 1927 J.C. Webster on its behalf attended a banquet at the Savoy Hotel in London on the bicentenary of the birth of General Wolfe, and ten years later Arthur Beauchesne was a delegate to an international congress of French writers in Paris. These casual representations were generalized in the request to the Massey Commission that the society take part in government delegations to international functions having to do with sciences and humanities. By the early 1970s reformers anticipated that the society, as Canada's national academy, should have an enlarged role in non-governmental international organizations.

In 1973, when a Standing Committee in International Relations had been set up, one advocate of regeneration drew these considerations together to highlight the third item of reform: 'This rationalization of the role of the Society as an academy, this acquisition of responsibility to air issues of importance, to aid the government of the day in its consideration of cultural and scientific problems, to act more visibly in international affairs, will require a more continuous presence on our part.' Meeting once a year may have been appropriate in 1882, but 'in our complex industrial society of 1973, a conscience must be active all 365 days of the year.'[19] Thus what was essential was a new 'corporate structure' to provide continuous operations. An executive secretary, Major Pierre Garneau, had been appointed in 1970, and he would come to know the labyrinthine networks within the society better than anyone, and throughout the 1970s proposals for extending the presidential term to three years and appointment of an executive director were vigorously debated. A three-year presidential term was instituted in 1978. These discussions were accompanied by establishment of standing committees in profusion sufficient to gratify the most obsessed academic devotees of meetings. Reform also expressed itself in a new vocabulary: an 'enhanced role' or raising the 'public profile' of the organization. More than one member was driven to the dictionary to find out the difference between society and academy.

These changes were driven forward by the Academy of Science (academy III). Academies I and II were passive or in the case of academy II opposed to such novelties as the three-year presidential term and an executive director. They seemed complaisant and content with the traditions of the past: one member of academy II donated a mace to the society to emphasize its ceremonial dignity. The task of suitably commemmorating the centenary of the society fell to the humanists, but the projected cultural history of Canada was never completed. One of the saddest moments in the history of the society occurred in 1975 when George Woodcock, founder of *Canadian Literature* and a prolific man of letters, resigned because he was unable to present himself for induction within three years of election and, according to the rules, would have his election declared null and void. Some members left no stone unturned to avoid this loss, but in the end Woodcock departed. 'I must,' he explained,

... recognize in myself a feeling of disappointment with membership in the Society. Had there been evidence of activities within the Society more exciting to me than its mere self-perpetuation, I would doubtless have thrown over other engagements to attend its meetings. But those activities never presented themselves, and when I did offer my services in connection with the one project that seemed to me of real importance, the preparation of a Cultural History of Canada, a task for which I am not without qualification, I received no reply that showed even the slightest interest in my participation. I have been left with the feeling that – though this was not so in the days of Lampman and his contemporaries – the presence of a mere author in the Society no longer has a great deal of relevance.

Woodcock was wrong about Lampman – the poet had dismissed the Royal Society as 'a useless and somewhat ludicrous institution' – but his remarks were symptomatic of more than just difficult personalities and insistence on rules being kept.[20]

8

Three Decades of Reform

Reform of the society did not work itself out in isolation but was profoundly affected by changes in Canadian society that virtually remade the country in the generation after 1960. Like other institutions the society was bombarded by the effects of the 'quiet revolution' in Quebec, unrest in the universities, the explosion of the numbers in academe, and an unsettling debate about science policy which threatened deeply entrenched beliefs about the nature of research and knowledge. The impact of these changes upon the society as an institution was comparable in magnitude to the great disjunction of the First World War.

The 1960s marked the beginnings of the breakup of a postwar consensus about the place of French Canada in national life. What began as an attempt to renovate Quebec society soon developed into what the Royal Commission on Bilingualism and Biculturalism in 1965 called the greatest crisis in the country's history. The Royal Society presented a brief to this commission (written by W.L. Morton and Maurice Lebel, who consulted some two hundred and fifty fellows) that supported bilingualism as a goal of public policy, argued that it should be realized first in the learned societies as well as in the civil service, and reiterated the notion that the society 'has always been a bilingual society. In the humanities, Section I is French,

Section II is English.'¹ As has been seen, however, bilingualism up to the 1950s was limited. Section I tended to be defensive about its autonomy, just as the province of Quebec insisted on provincial rights; section I represented French Canada and a rather passive accommodation to the rest of the society, just as Quebec seemed content with preservation of its culture, leaving to others control of economic life. The quiet revolution changed those views drastically: bilingualism was based on the idea of equality of 'two cultures' of two founding peoples, an old assumption in French Canada but a novel conception to nearly all Anglo-Canadians.

During the 1950s it became common practice for presidents, especially French Canadians, to give their addresses partly in French, partly in English, and in 1952 – for the first time since around 1921 – sections I and II held a joint session on the Massey Commission's report. There were joint sessions in 1953 on English and French studies in Canada, in 1954 on French settlement west of Lake Superior, and in 1956 on foreign languages and the progress of literature and sciences, the latter involving section V as well. Jean Bruchési in 1954, however, bluntly said that the division into two language sections was plausible in 1882 'owing to the fact that few ... in either of these sections were bilingual. It is doubtful whether the situation in 1954, though greatly improved, would, from a practical point of view, call for an amalgamation of both Sections; for bilingualism is not practised both ways; unfortunately it is too often a one-sided affair.' This was certainly the experience of French-speaking members of the science sections, who, if they wished to be understood by a fair proportion of their colleagues, hesitated to speak in their mother tongue.² Bruchési knew whereof he spoke: in 1950 section IV disapproved of a proposal that the assistant secretary treasurer should be bilingual, and in 1961 section I formally expressed its regret that the principal of McGill, Cyril James, in welcoming the society to his university, had slighted its bilingual character by not uttering a word of French.[3]

In the following decades such sensitivities and attitudes were to change slowly as the relations of French and English Canadians assumed the status of an almost permanent national crisis. Though there was greater determination to have the society live up to its bilingual nature – by, for example, having more joint meetings between the two humanities and social science academies, with a balance of papers in two languages – the *Transactions* of the three decades after 1960 reflects only partial success.

After 1960 the French-language academy experienced considerable change; in some respects both large and small the patterns of the past continued. Academy I maintained publication of *Présentations*, which from 1944 provided new members with a vehicle for making their talents more broadly known, and it served as a guardian of French-Canadian interests. The Pierre Chauveau medal was established by the society in 1951 'for distinguished contributions to knowledge in the humanities other than Canadian history and literature.' The medal was endowed by the province of Quebec, and initially all the members of the jury were from section I. Of the first 14 medals awarded 11 went to French Canadians; thereafter it was alternated more evenly.

Section I had a more varied composition than its English-language counterpart, which was becoming dominated by academics. Of the 65 members of section I in 1961, only 20 were in universities; 18 were government employees, 16 were authors and journalists, four were in business, and eight were priests, four of whom also taught in universities. There were also a few individuals from the worlds of music, theatre, and graphic arts. As the sociologist John Porter pointed out in 1965, section I was ethnically based rather than discipline based; almost a generation later two other observers were equally struck by the fact that this group was virtually all of French-Canadian origin. Some 84.1 per cent of an expanded membership had taken their first degrees in Quebec. This equation of section I with French Canada had been modified only slightly.[4] Harry Bernard, born in London, England, but educated (and assimilated) in French Quebec, editor of a Saint-Hyacinthe newspaper, was admitted to section I in 1943; Paul Wyczynski, a Pole and founder of the Centre for the Study of French Canadian Literature at the University of Ottawa, became a fellow in 1969, two years before Eva Kushner, a student of comparative literature and author of a book on St-Denys-Garneau. While the section in this way became more open, it narrowed in others. In 1987 there were only two members from outside Quebec, both from New Brunswick. After the death in 1967 of Donatien Frémont, a French-born journalist who published extensively on the Métis and the French of the west, a perspective once thought of crucial importance was lost in the section. The space of French Canadians contracted after 1960, and, increasingly referring to themselves as 'Québécois,' they ceased identifying with French-speaking people outside Quebec.

Section/academy I seemed a minuscule version of the new Quebec in other ways. As in the life of the province generally, the role of the clergy sharply declined from what had been a dominant presence as late as 1939. The prominence of Ottawa-based civil servants in conducting the relations of the academy with the other components of the society persisted, now reinforced by individuals from the bilingual University of Ottawa. The conspicuous position of the social sciences in Quebec universities since creation of a faculty of social sciences at Laval in the early 1940s was also reflected in the society.

The rise of the social sciences in French Canada was closely tied to the quiet revolution, and the work of Jean-Charles Falardeau, Albert Faucher, and Father Georges-Henri Lévesque (all of whom became members of the

Royal Society) marked a profound break from the way Quebec society had been understood before the war. The historian Fernand Ouellet, who taught at Laval, Carleton, and Ottawa, was elected a member in 1967, and served as secretary of the society 1977–80, had recast the social and economic history of Quebec into a new perspective and explained the origins of French-Canadian nationalism as a reactionary response to economic crisis in the early nineteenth century. He was also a stringent critic of those forces that had impeded the growth of history as a social science in his native province. The French Canadians who became presidents of the society after 1960 were themselves symbols of the new Quebec. Three were scientists (Léo Marion, Léon Lortie, and Claude Fortier of the medical school at Laval), Marc-Adélard Tremblay was an anthropologist, and Jules Deschênes was a jurist. There was a special Quebec resonance to Lortie's presidential address in 1969, delivered at the moment when humans walked on the moon, in which he dealt with the old opposition to science and said that it had won out over classical humanism.[5]

There was a tendency in academy I, as in old section I, for members to identify with Canada as a whole rather than with Quebec nationalism, which took a separatist turn in 1976. Pierre Trudeau, a critic of French-Canadian nationalism, indeed of all nationalisms, had been nominated for fellowship in 1963 by Bruchési, Daviault, and Sylvestre, who referred to his prowess in judo.[6] In general academy I sympathized with Trudeau liberalism and its attempt to remake Canada – and by implication the Royal Society – into a more hospitable and equal place for French Canadians.

Members of the Royal Society were directly exposed to turmoil and confusion in the universities after the mid-1960s because so many of them were academics. The student protests against authority, bureaucracy, and elitism, as well as the hypocrisy of their elders, challenged the essential values that the society embodied. Hardly an article in the *Transactions* in the late 1960s and throughout the 1970s did not either deplore this upsurge of so-called barbarism or attempt to explain it. Maurice Lebel thought students in general confused by the swift pace of contemporary change. They 'find it most difficult not only to adjust to the new order, but also to interest themselves in the past and to visualize a society different from theirs. They do not know anything, and, what is more, they often refuse to know anything, about the cultural background and foundations of contemporary civilization. Hence the more or less complete rupture with the past.'[7] The sociologist S.D. Clark devoted his presidential address in 1976 to the attack on authority structures in Canadian society and the erosion of values that had supported pursuit of knowledge. The student rebellion coincided with, and to some degree expressed, broader and growing uneasiness with environmental degradation, depletion of non-renewable resources, the computer and information banks, and loss of privacy. The philosopher George Grant attracted a considerable following for questioning the whole thrust of Western technological progress and for defending philosophy as a quest for moral truth. The time had long passed when Steacie had dismissed loose talk about the moral responsibility of scientists for nuclear weapons by saying that all scientists can do is increase natural knowledge and potential for control and what society does with this power is a political matter. For some, science and technology had become part of the problem. This upsurge of discontent and criticism was paralleled by the rise of the second wave of the women's movement, which threw into sharp relief the minute representation of women in the society and its failure to live up to the decision of 1913. In time the very words 'Fellow' and 'Fellowship' would be read in a context radically different from what had been taken for granted.

Expansion of the universities to cope with the baby boom enlarged the professoriate and compounded the problems of the Royal Society in representing certain fields. Between 1960 and 1970 the number of social science professors quadrupled from 1,939 to 8,516[8] and raised again the issue of the social sciences in section/academy II. This growth occurred chiefly in economics, political science, psychology, and sociology. 'There are today in Section II,' said S.D. Clark in 1974, '44 social scientists. At least 20 of them are over 65 years of age, many were over seventy and no longer participating in scholarly activities.' According to him sociology in particular was ludicrously underrepresented. There were 600 sociologists in English Canada, but only three were in academy II in 1977. What concerned Clark was not only that the society was failing to represent the interests of social scientists but that its image did not encourage respect for the society in the minds of those younger scholars who were 'very much caught up in the democratic, non-elitist, ethos which has developed so strongly in recent years.'[9] Nor did it quite fit the requirements of a more active role for the society as a whole that was being discussed at this time. Academy II, which had 150 members, half of them over 65 years of age, sought to elect 36 younger fellows in addition to the 10 that it was entitled to under the existing rules. The council compromised and allowed academy I to add 10; II, 20; and III, 34. In the period 1961–78 the total membership of the society increased from 543 to 850 for this and other reasons.

For most scientists in academy III the unsettling effects of campus unrest and the quiet revolution paled in comparison with the decision of the Liberal government in the mid-1960s to articulate a science policy for the country.

Establishment of a Science Secretariat in the Privy Council Office in 1964, of the Science Council of Canada in 1966, and of the Ministry of State for Science and Technology in 1971 was accompanied by widespread and intense discussion within the Canadian and international scientific communities and within the Royal Society. Canada had supported scientific research through the NRC and such bodies as the Defence Research Board and Atomic Energy Control Board for many years; the problem that arose at this time was whether the state ought to favour multidisciplinary, large-scale 'mission-oriented' research projects that would support national social and economic goals in such areas as water resources, space, nuclear power, computer application, and technical aid to developing countries.

Senator Maurice Lamontagne, who chaired the Senate Special Committee on Science Policy, which sat for five years and issued three comprehensive reports, told a symposium of the Royal Society in 1969 that the scientist was under attack from two fronts – 'criticized by the politician for being sterile in terms of practical results and by the rebels for being a menace to society because of his too great technological achievements.' The growing expense of scientific research, moreover, made it essential to set priorities. 'The scientist will have to accept the fact that research has become a political activity in the noblest sense of that expression, that it must be guided by national goals and subjected to a systematic policy review in the light of these objectives.' He added in Trudeauesque language, 'what goes on in the scientist's bedroom is very much the business of the politician.'[10] This new partnership between government and science was declared to be the beginning of a 'new era' – a phrase last used in the reformist days of the War of 1914–18.

The natural sciences were not alone in being summoned to serve society directly. Arthur J.R. Smith, chair of the Economic Council of Canada, expanded on the necessity

for more 'policy-directed research for helping solve problems or achieve goals' on the part of the social sciences.
While he recognized that social scientists had recently conducted research of political importance in the areas of
bilingualism and biculturalism, industrial relations, and
Aboriginal policy, he anticipated a more continuous, for-
malized, and directed effort.[11]

This new departure in science policy impinged on the
Royal Society in two ways. First, it triggered far-reaching
debate among scientists that dominated the business of
academy III from the mid-1960s and throughout the 1970s.
The idea of socially relevant research ran up against a
deeply engrained tradition within the NRC and the universities that emphasized 'basic research' motivated by
curiosity and the intellectual interests of scientists themselves. To critics, the new policies – or rather expectations
– were based on profound misunderstanding of how
scientists actually operated and, by isolating certain spe-
cialties for support, threatened others. The entire exercise
of holding extended public hearings on science, moreover, had uncovered, if it had not actually stimulated, an
undercurrent of hostility to science and scientists. 'By
exploiting the public resentment of constant change and
perhaps its fear of a technological takeover by machines
and the men who run them, the cost of scientific research
can be put in an unfavourable light, and the scientist can
be blamed as directly and solely responsible for such things
as overcrowding, pollution, and the nuclear menace.'[12]
Gerhard Herzberg, one of the few refugee intellectuals
who had managed to find safety in Canada in the late
1930s, stressed 'the need for basic research as a cultural
activity of the same type as literature, art, and music' and
noted that while it was common to deplore lack of freedom of intellectuals behind the Iron Curtain it was less
appreciated that scientists in the West must be given the
same intellectual freedom as writers, artists, and com-

posers. 'It is they and they alone,' he said of scientists, 'who can appreciate what is significant and worth doing in science.'[13]

This anxiety about the state defining the objectives for scholars was shared by some social scientists and historians. Back in 1951 in a paper prepared for the Massey Commission S.D. Clark and the economist Burton S. Kierstead had expressed reservations about the creation of a government agency for the social sciences located in Ottawa and modelled on the NRC. 'We fear less the danger of propaganda or of interference with a scholar's freedom to publish his conclusions, though this danger exists, than that such a council would direct and divert scholarly energies to non-scientific problems, or to problems of only secondary interest.'[14] This issue had always been the bugbear of Harold Innis, and years later Clark was faithful to his friend's convictions when he opposed efforts within the Royal Society to remake it into an institution of immediate use to the state and dependent on it.

Second, the initiatives in science policy provided the Royal Society with an opportunity to assert a long-awaited role. It was invited to participate in 1963 in formulation of science policy, and it presented briefs to the minister of industry in 1965 and to the Special Senate Committee on Science Policy in 1969. The society supported creation of the Science Council and in 1969 advocated greater expenditure for research in the natural sciences as well as in the humanities and social sciences, which were, it asserted, of direct usefulness both in resolving tensions between French and English ('We have ... a common culture in this country which needs only to be discovered and acknowledged.') and in dissipating widespread uneasiness about the materialism of science.[15] A storm of paper was generated by the possibility that the society would finally find a niche in national policy, and the organization was greatly encouraged by the recommendation of the Senate Com-

mittee that it be given overall responsibility for developing and maintaining relations with foreign private scientific and engineering bodies.

The remaking of the Royal Society into a national academy, which took up most of the 1980s, was the consequence of profound changes in the social and intellectual
environment as well as determined efforts by reformers
in academy III to turn it into something more than an
'academic hall of fame.' During that decade a succession
of symposia explored the worldwide crisis over acid rain,
depletion of energy resources, and nuclear winter, and
these concerns ultimately led to a comprehensive approach
to global change. Thanks partly to Kenneth Hare the society also undertook contract work for federal government
departments evaluating research programs on air pollutants, health effects of lead in the environment, and AIDS,
and, for the Ontario government, a nuclear safety review.
(See Appendix, part D.)

Scientists had become conscious of how dramatically
the 'public image of science' had altered since the late
1960s, as reflected in the decline in enrolments in natural
sciences, engineering, and mathematics in the universities,[16] and in 1982 academy III began a program aimed at
correcting mistaken popular impressions and improving
science education in schools and universities. Amendments
to the society's by-laws were a constant preoccupation
and an indication of a drive to correct the mistakes of
history: academies II and III were enjoined when electing
new members 'to ensure representation by regions, and
female scientists and researchers, and from smaller institutions. Academy III is also to ensure that a greater number of representatives of Francophone scientists are considered for election.'[17]

An uncharacteristic note of brisk vitality animated these
activities, and the pace of change quickened. In 1989 the

minister of state for science and technology announced a grant to the society of $1 million a year for five years to support its proposals to improve public awareness of science, advance the status of women in scholarship, and evaluate research in Canada. This support, however, was made conditional on the society's addressing 'administrative urgencies' in order to make it more effective in its new role and also encouraging women's participation in the natural sciences and engineering fields and accelerating their election to the society.[18] With the aid of a firm of consultants, the society adopted a corporate action plan, designed in part to 'enhance its public profile,' revamped its structure, and began raising funds in a more determined fashion. In 1992 the annual budget was $2.3 million, with income from provincial governments, corporations, research councils, and government departments almost equalling the grant of $1 million from the Ministry of State for Science and Technology.

In the four years after 1989 the secretariat staff increased from six to 21, five of whom were working on the Global Change program. Ancient hopes regarding a permanent headquarters, preferably in a prestigious location in Ottawa, were rekindled.[19]

By the early 1990s the Royal Society was being transformed by the initiatives of academy III, which had nearly two-thirds of the members – 789 – compared to academy I, with 183, and academy II, with 365. Between 1989 and 1992, 47 women were elected to the society, bringing female representation to 91 out of a total of 1,337. Old section III had throughout the institution's history been a force for change, especially in the three decades after 1900, and this role was reasserted by academy III after 1980. The subjects of the society's new 'mission' tended to fall into the scientific realms, even though involvement of social scientists and humanists was anticipated and encouraged. Academies I and II were in a sense bystanders in

this shift in direction, and people who spoke on their behalf expressed misgivings about the swiftness of change
and pleaded that their academies not be ignored.

The 'new' Royal Society projected its fresh image in a
glossy 'Profile of the National Academy' (1990), which
constitutes a crucial document in its history. The keynote
is the society's considerable influence in the past and cen-
trality in the future as a national academy. Photographs
include those of Gerhard Herzberg and John Polanyi, who
received the Nobel Prize for chemistry in 1971 and 1986,
respectively; the diplomat George Ignatieff, the literary
critic Northrop Frye, and two leading reformers, the geologist Digby J. McLaren and F. Kenneth Hare; the novelists Margaret Atwood, Marie-Claire Blais, and Antonine
Maillet; and Alice Wilson, the first women elected to the
society. Apart from the traditional claim that the society
promoted establishment of a whole galaxy of national scientific and cultural institutions (on which more later) and
a quotation from its Act of Incorporation, a sense of the
society's actual past is only faintly conveyed. The past is
irrelevant. When the minister of state for industry, science, and technology announced the grant of 1989 he said
that 'while yours is a tradition worthy of recognition, it
had little bearing on our decision to provide you with
funding.' The government was investing in the future,
not in what had been.

Much earlier, E.W. Steacie had warned the society of
the dangers to the freedom of research posed by benefac-
tors, and he approvingly quoted Leacock to the effect that
the only good ones were dead. A live benefactor, said
Steacie, whether an individual, corporation, or government, 'is always just around the corner.' In 1994 the society found out what was around the corner. A consulting
firm, commissioned by Industry, Science and Technology,
now Industry Canada, appraised its performance in three
areas supported by the $1 million annual grant – women

in scholarship, public awareness of science, and evaluation of research – and found it medium in the first two and disappointing in the third. (The society's report of 1991, *Realizing the Potential: A Strategy for University Research in Canada*, which itself cost over $1.2 million to produce, unsurprisingly called for a vast increase of public expenditure on research.) The consultants also found that the grant provided nearly 70 per cent of the society's operational budget. Partly as a result of this report Industry Canada drastically reduced its support, precipitating a fiscal crisis in the society that is still unresolved.[20]

Even before this turn of events it was clear the the reform and revitalization of the Royal Society had only partially overcome the malaise of the old organization. Problems persist because as a national institution the society reflects the character of a country whose own quandaries are never resolved with finality. A French-Canadian, or Québécois member, on hearing the phrase 'two cultures' would think of French and English relations; a scientist would associate the words with C.P. Snow's distinctions between the cultures of science and the humanities. As has been seen, both themes were of persistent and cumulative importance in the old society, and they continue to be so in the new. In some ways the changes since the late 1980s have accentuated the minority position of Québécois in the society. This is more than a matter of numbers; one objective of the new society is still to make bilingualism more prominent in its functions, and in 1990 President Deschênes pleaded for 'a fairer balance between French and English in the composition of the Society ... The French-speaking scientific community is not lacking in numbers.'[21]

Older habits continue also in the very unequal interest and involvement among members in the society's affairs: poor attendance at meetings has always been a problem but could hardly now be attributed to difficulties of travel.

One fellow estimated – without being contradicted – attendance in 1986 at only 10 per cent of total membership.[22] The consultants who appraised the society in 1993 were surprised when a survey of 60 randomly selected fellows elicited such a low response rate as to be not 'statistically meaningful.' This indicates, apart from apathy, that for many people fellowship in the Royal Society is seen as an honour entailing few if any obligations.

It has been observed above that section II exhibited a conservatism in the 1920s and later in the Cold War period with its defence of the Western humanistic traditions. In 1965 the sociologist John Porter was struck by the virtually complete 'lack of articulation' between the members of section II and the political system and attributed this 'depoliticizing of the higher learning' to the influence of Harold Innis. From the outset, however, the old society had deliberately distanced itself from political issues; after all, it could hardly afford to irritate politicians who provided its funds. This lack of social criticism and political activism – which Porter thought normal for intellectuals – became all the more surprising in the decades after 1965, when a highly adversarial social criticism developed in the social sciences and historical writing, little of which was reflected in academy II.[23]

Porter noticed other features of that group which were to endure with slight modification. Some 85 of 104 members in 1961 were in universities, 37 (43 per cent) at the University of Toronto. Almost one-third of his sample of 88 had been born outside Canada, mostly in the United Kingdom. Almost a generation later 31 per cent of fellows in academy II held appointments at Toronto. Because of universities' recruitment of Americans during the 1960s and 1970s – the society went on record as opposing any legislative impediments to open hiring – the proportion of fellows with senior degrees from the United Kingdom fell. Those with American ones constituted 38.1 per cent of the total in academy II, and those with Canadian degrees 30.3 per cent. In a period when the provinces were asserting their powers against centralist domination and regional attachments were deepening, the belief that memberships in the Royal Society should be spread more evenly rose accordingly. George Lawson in the 1880s had worried about centralization and 'fair representation' of provinces and he would have understood the renewed emphasis on recruitment from 'the regions' and smaller institutions.

Lawson and his contemporaries would also recognize something familiar about the essentials of the global change program and the efforts to enhance public awareness of science. The first in some ways reverts to the long-standing concern with conservation that was so conspicuous in the first generation of the society. Lawson and his generation, moreover, had also devoted themselves to advancing appreciation for 'science culture' among the public, and some were pioneers of 'nature study' in the schools. They were succeeded by advocates of the research ideal and recognition of science as at least the equal of the old classical humanism. The society's decision in the 1980s to declare 'creationism' unfit to be taught along with evolution in schools also harks back to issues present at its beginnings. In this and in other ways the new national academy carries over traits of the old Victorian Royal Society of Canada.

9

Reflections

The Royal Society of Canada has served many purposes and discharged its mandate to encourage the sciences and humanities in different ways. In the days of William Dawson and John G. Bourinot the society was seen as a centre of authority and a working organization as distinct from a purely honorary one. Both men accepted as its main task the publication of the *Transactions*, containing the best scientific papers and reflecting the entire range of intellectual activity in the country. There was a commodiousness to this publication, and a receptivity to the work of many people who were not fellows of the society, including the exceptional cases of some chiefs of the Six Nations, Nova Scotia schoolchildren, and Frank Roe, the locomotive engineer who became an expert on the history of the prairie bison. Before 1920 there was no Canadian alternative for publication of articles in history or in chemistry and physics. J.B. Brebner, who had harsh words for the society in 1945, was more positive later in saying that in its first generation it 'succeeded remarkably well ... in winning the loyalties of the most zealous and mature scholars, and its early transactions contained a respectable share of the best work that was being done in Canada.'[1]

This first generation encountered problems that were to become enduring patterns, notably the contrast between the membership at large and the relatively small number at the centre who oversaw its administration and who often were the most devoted contributors to its journal. Over time the society honoured the most deserving scholars in the country; its evolution as an institution, however, owed most to such individuals as John George Bourinot, Benjamin Sulte, Léon Gérin, William F. Ganong, John C. McLennan, Lawrence J. Burpee, and Maurice Lebel. The list of nominal fellows is much larger – from Goldwin Smith and John Watson, abbé Lionel Groulx and Donald Creighton, to Marshall McLuhan. The society derived prestige from these names – an important consideration for an institution that dealt in prestige – but little else except membership dues. Apathy and poor attendance at meetings have always been features of the society. As early as 1920 it was clearly evident that there was a contradiction between requiring at least a paper from each fellow every three years and the inability of the society to publish all that it received. The presence in the Royal Society of people who were important in Canadian intellectual life is no doubt significant for the history of the society. It was, however, in many cases of small consequence in those individuals' own lives. Indeed, it is striking how seldom biographers of even such relatively active fellows as Robert Falconer, John Macoun, E.W.R. Steacie, or the poet E.J. Pratt made anything more of their membership than the recognition and honour bestowed on their subjects.[2]

Sectional boundaries were part of the society from the beginning, but the rise of laboratory research accentuated the breach between the sciences and humanities and indeed among the sciences themselves. Between 1900 and 1930 the society and the *Transactions* were vehicles by which the sciences in section III, mainly physics and chemistry, and the biological sciences in section V, established a professional status. The Great War, by equating patriotism with scientific research and efficiency, hastened the creation of the NRC and shifted the initiative within the society to the scientists who grew to dominate its mem-

bership. In the inter-war years section III promoted reform and, in a curious parallel to the Progressive party in
national politics, tried to democratize membership. This
spasm of reform was frustrated partially by the structures
that coupled the sciences with the two increasingly conservative humanities sections, neither of which proved
very receptive to making membership more inclusive or
welcoming new forms of knowledge.

After 1930 and definitely by 1950 the *Transactions* played
only a minor role in publication of Canadian research in
the sciences and humanities. Special ideological conditions
after the Second World War lent support to the idea of
symposia that would transcend disciplines. Many of the
humanists wanted to defend western values against the
Cold War enemy; some scientists were reacting against
hyper-specialization and, later, responding to demands
for 'relevance' and accountablility in the science policy
debate. Just as in the late nineteenth century the society
had seen itself as a point of contact for geographically
dispersed scholars, a century later it was dedicated to
overcoming the barriers that its own members had helped
create.

The society has always represented more than individual
intellectual achievement: membership was invariably
looked on in terms of regions and provinces, new fields,
including the troublesome case of the social sciences, and,
much later, gender. We have seen that in coping with
emergence of new fields the society invariably expanded
membership despite criticism since the 1920s that it was
already too large and that, in the words of Lorne Pierce, it
was becoming what the founders had hardly intended,
an 'inter university faculty club.' The identification of
fellowship with factors other than distinction was present
at the beginning with the establishment of section I and
the separation of humanists along language and, as time
revealed, ethnic lines.

Daniel Wilson and Arthur Beauchesne inside the soci-

ety, and critics outside it, regreted this division for per-
petuating the isolation that Lorne had hoped to surmount.[3]
This separation was reinforced by the long term effects of
the relative neglect of science in late Victorian French
Canada. This division within the Royal Society was repli-
cated in other organizations: the Canadian Historical Association and the *Canadian Historical Review* had been
Anglo-Canadian in character; after 1947 the *Revue d'histoire
de l'Amérique française* was predominantly French Canadian, and very few individuals contributed to both. Though
in the society the sectionalizing of the two language groups
was challenged by Benjamin Sulte, Marius Barbeau, and
others, two recent observers exaggerated only a little in
concluding that as far as the Royal Society is concerned 'a
separation has long since taken place in the intellectual
elite of overall Canadian society.'[4] The Royal Society did
not create this situation; however, by institutionalizing
division it helped perpetuate an intellectual separatism.

Through all its permutations there have been two enduring features of the society. The first was the priority
given to recognizing distinction and the deep attachment
of the fellows to preserving their pre-eminence. The notion that distinctions and awards were an actual incentive
to excel was deeply imbedded in Victorian culture, and
this belief was consistently perpetuated by the society.
The closest it ever came to questioning the very principle
of limited membership was in the inter-war discussion
over 'associate' fellows when some scientists saw clearly
that exclusivity impeded the scientific sections in bringing together in a vital society all who were actively engaged in research. The society never resolved this dilemma
and never questioned outright the concept of honour on
which it was based. In fact in 1927 and 1946 it urged the
government to establish a Canadian Order of Merit for
conspicuous public service and intellectual leadership.

This preoccupation with honour was intertwined with
a recurrent feeling that the society and its members were

insufficiently appreciated by public and government, a refrain that punctuated many ruminations on the status of the institution. 'Academically this was the top,' Arthur Lower recalled of his election, 'and from the top the only direction is down. Unfortunately the Royal Society, our senior academic society, is little known to our citizens and has little prestige. Canadians being more interested in American big-league baseball than in intellectual distinction, there is no prospect of the situation changing.'[5] It has always been easier to attribute this indifference to defective public relations or a populist anti-intellectualism than to take a cold, hard look at the society itself.

Brebner made light of what was evoked by the initials 'FRSC,' but with domination of the society by university professors membership became a prized academic honour. In some quarters fellowship in the Royal Society was taken as an index of the real as distinct from the nominal professoriate in the country. When the philosopher George Grant was elected to the society his attitude towards it was one of 'respect' – respect for those who were in it and for those who had gone before. This reverence, however, did not inhibit him from privately telling jokes about holding open the door of the men's room after a session for his elders whose needs were more urgent than his own.[6]

The second strand that runs throughout the society's history was the search for a place in the country beyond simply encouraging scholarship and bestowing honours. That the society contained expertise and experience in so many fields made it seem inevitable that it would become the source of advice to governments, an expectation that was encouraged, in the early years, by observation of the activities of similar societies in other countries. These hopes, however, never materialized in its first century. The society made repeated representations to the state on many subjects – sometimes, as in its submission to the Massey Commission, urging a more extended role for itself. The opportunities for establishing a niche that involved direct influence, however, progressively narrowed as the state created its own scientific institutions and granting agencies. Yet an important feature of the society's sense of itself has been the belief that in the past it has been

more or less instrumental in bringing about the establishment of such important national institutions as the Public Archives, the National Gallery, the National Museum, the Topographical and Geodetic Surveys, the Meteorological Service, the Hydrographic Service, the National Research Council, the Historic Sites and Monuments Board, the Geographic Board, the Dominion Observatory, the Experimental Farms, the National Parks, and through its members has taken an active part in the organization of the Canadian Historical Association, the Canadian Geographical Society, Canadian Political Science Association, and many other similar organizations in the fields of history, literature and science.[7]

Since these claims were made in 1936 the list of institutions has grown longer and includes the National Library and the Canada Council. What the society accomplished in the past always encouraged aspirations as to what it might achieve in the future; yet an exaggerated view of its own historical influence could also exacerbate a feeling of dissatisfaction with its present impotence. The more closely the decisions to create individual institutions are examined the clearer it is that the society as an institution, as distinct from individuals who happened to be members of it, was not decisive, and in many cases it was peripheral. There is no doubt that the society supported these creations; the issue is confused, however, by claiming for the institution influence that lay with individuals in whose lives the society occupied a small place. The Royal Society has always been considerably less than the sum of its parts.

Appendix

Publications

Since the mid-1950s the Royal Society of Canada has issued four series of books, most of them edited collections, intended to reach a wider audience than its *Transactions*.

A   Special Publications, from 1956

The Grenville Problem, ed. James E. Thompson (1956)
The Proterozoic in Canada, ed. James E. Gill (1957)
Soils in Canada, ed. Robert F. Legget (1961)
Tectonics of the Canadian Shield, ed. J.S. Stevenson (1962)
Marine Distribution, ed. M.J. Dunbar (1963)
Studies in Analytical Geochemistry, ed. Denis M. Shaw (1963)
Crucial Maps in the Early Cartography and Place-Nomenclature of the Atlantic Coast of Canada, ed. W.F. Ganong, with Introductory Commentary and Map Notes by Theodore E. Layng (1964)
Geochronology in Canada, ed. F. Fitz Osborne (1964)
Appalachian Tectonics, ed. T.H. Clark (1967)
Continental Drift, ed. G.D. Garland (1968)
The Earth Sciences in Canada: A Centennial Appraisal and Forecast, ed. E.R.W. Neale (1968)
Energy Flow – Its Biological Dimensions (The IBP in Canada 1964–1974), ed. T.W.M. Cameron and L.W. Billingsley (1975)
Glacial Till – An Interdisciplinary Study, ed. Robert F. Leggett (1976)

Nuclear Issues in the Canadian Energy Context, ed. E.P. Hincks
(1979)
*Nuclear Winter and Associated Effects: A Canadian Appraisal of
the Environmental Impact of Nuclear War*, ed. F.K. Hare and
A. Forester (1985)
Planet under Stress: The Challenge of Global Change, ed.
Constance Mungall and Digby J. McLaren (1990)
Claiming the Future:Women in Scholarship, ed. Elizabeth May
and Frances G. Halpenny (1991)

B   Studia Varia, 1957–70

Studia Varia, ed. E.G.D. Murray (1957)
Our Debt to the Future, ed. E.G.D. Murray (1958)
The Canadian Northwest: Its Potentialities, ed. Frank H. Underhill
(1959)
Evolution: Its Science and Doctrine, ed. T.W.M. Cameron (1960)
Aux sources du présent, ed. Léon Lortie and Adrien Plouffe
(1960)
Canadian Universities Today, ed. George F.G. Stanley and
Guy Sylvestre (1961)
Canadian Population and Northern Colonization, ed. V.W. Bladen
(1962)
Higher Education in a Changing Canada, ed. J.E. Hodgetts (1966)
Pioneers of Canadian Science, ed. G.F.G. Stanley (1966)
Structures sociales du Canada français, ed. Guy Sylvestre (1966)
Scholarship in Canada 1967: Achievement and Outlook, ed.
R.H. Hubbard (1967)
Water Resources of Canada, ed. C.E. Dolman (1967)
Le Canada français d'aujourd'hui, ed. L. Lamontagne (1970)
Visages de la civilisation au Canada français, ed. L. Lamontagne
(1970)

C   Proceedings of Symposia, from 1970

The Tundra Environment, ed. F. Kenneth Hare (1970)
Mercury in Man's Environment, ed. J.E. Watkin (1971)

Communications into the Home, ed. W.C. Brown (1972)
Futures Canada, ed. J.T. Wilson (1973)
Physics and Chemistry on Ice, ed. F. Whalley, S.J. Jones, and
    L.W. Gold (1973)
Energy Resources, ed. K.J. Laidler (1973)
Copernicus, ed. P. Wyczynski (1973)
Waste Recycling and the Environment, ed. P. Reynolds (1974)
Le Rapport Parent, dix ans après, ed. L.-P. Audet (1975)
Frontiers and Limitations of Knowledge, ed. C. Fortier (1975)
Preserving the Canadian Heritage, ed. K.J. Laidler (1975)
The Patterns of Amerindian Identity, ed. M.-A. Tremblay (1976)
Problems of Development in Atlantic Canada, ed. S.D. Clark (1976)
The University of the Future, ed. Jan Morgan and K.J. Laidler
    (1976)
New Perspectives in Canadian Archaeology, ed. A.G. McKay (1976)
Canada and World Food, ed. W.S. Henderson (1977)
Shifts in the Balance of Canada's Resource Endowments, ed.
    R.E. Folinsbee (1977)
Parasites, Their World and Ours, ed. A.M. Fallis (1977)
Planetary Atmospheres, ed. A. Vallance Jones (1977)
*Hermes (The Communications Technology Satellite): Its Perfor-
    mance and Applications,* 3 vols, ed. I. Paghis (1978)
Glacier Beds: The Ice-Rock Interface, as vol. 23 no. 89 (1979);
    published and sold by the International Glaciological
    Society, Cambridge, England
The Written Word, ed. A.G. McKay (1980)
A Century of Canada's Arctic Islands, 1880–1980, ed. Morris
    Zaslow (1981)
Ethanol from Biomass, ed. H.E. Duckworth and E.A. Thompson
    (1983)
*Risk: The Assessment and Perception of Risk to Human Health in
    Canada,* ed. J.T. Rogers and D.V. Bates (1983)
Renewals in the Theory of Literary History, ed. Eva Kushner (1983)
Continuité et rupture. Les sciences sociales au Québec, 2 vols,
    ed. Georges-Henri Lévesque et al. (1984)
*The Information Economy: Its Implications for Canada's Industrial
    Strategy,* ed. C.C. Gotlieb (1985)

Origin and Evolution of the Universe: Evidence for Design?, ed.
J.M. Robson (1987)
Symbols in Life and Art, ed. James A. Leith (1987)
The Family in Crisis: A Population Crisis?, eds. Jacques Légaré,
Roderic Beaujot, and T.R. Balakrishnan (1989)
Equity, Fiduciaries and Trusts, ed. T.G. Youdan (1989)
Diet, Nutrition and Health, ed. K.K. Carroll (1990)
Facing the Demographic Future, ed. Roderic Beaujot (1990)
One Step Forward, Two Steps Back?, ed. Susan Mann
Trofimenkoff (1990)
New Reproductive Technologies: Where Are We Heading?
Video, n.d.

D   Reports on Studies Carried Out by the Society, from 1983

Acid Deposition in North America, ed. F.K. Hare (1983)
Long-range Transport of Airborne Pollutants in North America,
ed. F.K. Hare (1984)
*The Great Lakes Water Quality Agreement: An Evolving Instrument
for Ecosystem Management*, eds. O.L. Loucks and H.A. Regier
(1985)
Lead in Gasoline: A Review of the Canadian Policy Issue, ed.
F.K. Hare (1985)
Lead in Gasoline: Alternatives to Lead in Gasoline, ed. F.K. Hare
(1986)
*Lead in the Canadian Environment: Science and Regulation (Final
Report)*, ed. F.K. Hare (1986)
*Global Change: The Candian Opportunity, Canadian Global Change
Program Report No. 1*, ed. William S. Fyfe (1986)
*Human Dimensions of Global Change: The Challenge to the
Humanities and Social Sciences*, eds. D. Braybrooke and
Gilles Paquet (1987)
*The Safety of Ontario's Nuclear Power Reactors: A Scientific and
Technical Review*, ed. F.K. Hare (1988)
*AIDS: A Perspective for Canadians (Summary Report and Recom-
mendations)*, ed. M. Chrétien (1988)
AIDS: A Perspective for Canadians (Background Papers), ed.
M. Chrétien (1988)

Understanding AIDS: A Canadian Strategy, ed. D. Spurgeon
(1988)

*Review of Studies of Health Effects of Long Range Transport of Air
Pollutants*, eds. P.T. Macklem, D.V. Bates, J. Hanley, and
P. Lioy (1988)

Science and the Public, ed. E.R. Ward Neale (1988)

The Canadian Global Change Program: A Progress Report, Canadian
Global Change Program Report (1988)

Canada and the Changing Atmosphere, ed. F.K. Hare (1989)

*Contribution of Satellite Observations to the Canadian Global
Change Program*, Canadian Global Change Program Report
(1989)

A Study of University Research in Canada: The Issues, Committee
on University Research (1989)

Plan for Advancement of Women in Scholarship, Committee for
Advancement of Women (1989)

Plan for the Evaluation of Research in Canada, Advisory Committee for Evaluation of Research in Canada (1989)

Tobacco, Nicotine, and Addiction (1989)

Communicating Science: Why and How, David Spurgeon (1990)

*Carbon Dioxide Emission Reduction Potential in the Industrial
Sector*, ed. L.D. Danny Harvey (1990)

Boreas: Boreal Forest Experiment Report, Canadian Global Change
Program Report, ed. Josef Chilar (1990)

*Canada's Relations with the International Council of Scientific
Unions (ICSU): Final Report*, ed. Paul H. LeBlond (1991)

*Realizing the Potential: A Strategy for University Research in
Canada*, University Research Committee (1991)

Public Awareness of Science Program: A National Action Plan,
National Committee for the Public Awareness of Science
(1991)

*Expected Reduction in Damage to Canadian Lakes under Legislated
and Proposed Decreases in Sulphur Dioxide Emissions*, Committee on Lake Acidification of the Canadian Global Change
Program (1992)

Notes

Preface

1 This study is based chiefly on the *Proceedings and Transactions of the Royal Society of Canada. Mémoires et Comptes rendus de la Société royale du Canada*, which has been published each year since 1882. For the sake of brevity all references to this journal have been abbreviated as follows: P denotes Proceedings, T, Transactions, followed by the year of the meeting, which was not invariably the date of publication. For most of the period the transactions, like the society, were divided into sections, S, which are numbered I to V.

The other basis of this account is the Royal Society of Canada Papers in the National Archives of Canada (NA) – MG 28 I 458 – abbreviated RSC Papers. This collection of 107 boxes is uneven and heavily weighted to the post-1960 years.

Chapter One Origins and Early Character, 1882–1914

1 Robert M. Stamp, *Royal Rebels: Princess Louise and the Marquis of Lorne* (Toronto, 1988)
2 Bourinot, *The Intellectual Development of the Canadian People* (Toronto, 1881)

3 Morgan, *The Dominion Annual Register and Review for 1881* (Toronto, 1882)
4 Canada, *House of Commons Debates*, 19 March 1883, 263
5 NA, George M. Grant Papers, G. Stewart to Grant, 18 March 1885
6 *Bystander*, 1883, 67
7 *House of Commons Debates*, 14 May 1883, 1195; *The Week* VII (6 June 1890), 418
8 N.F. Davin, *The Secretary of the Royal Society: A Literary Fraud* (Ottawa, 1882); J.E. Collins, *Canada under the Administration of Lord Lorne* (Toronto, 1884), 363.
9 J.W. Dawson, *Fifty Years of Work in Canada* (London, 1901), 178–9; McGill University Archives, J.W. Dawson Papers, Wilson to Dawson, 8 Dec. 1881. In his report to Lorne, Dawson said that while there was equality between the literary sections, 'no distinctions of race or language were admitted in the other sections,' and he indicated that the French objected strongly to naming the organization an academy or institute but all seemed satisfied with 'Royal Society of Canada.' Dawson to Lorne, 2 Jan. 1882
10 P, 1882, V–XI
11 Royal Society of Canada, *Fifty Years Retrospect: Canada 1882–1932* (Toronto, 1932), 58
12 Robin Harris, *A History of Higher Education in Canada, 1663–1960* (Toronto, 1976), 98
13 P, 1887, VII
14 RSC Papers, Box 26, File 'Section IV Coresp., 1910–1911,' J.J. Mackenzie to A.H. MacKay, 24 Feb. 1911
15 P, 1899, X
16 P, 1889, XVII–XVIII; P, 1893, II
17 Queen's University Archives, Charles Mair Papers, W.D. Lighthall to Mair, 8 March 1889
18 P, 1901, VIII
19 P, 1894, IX
20 P, 1890, VII
21 RSC Papers, Box 1, 'Minutes of Council from 1908 to 1916,' 28 Feb. 1910

22 P, 1895, III; P, 1909, VI; P, 1892, XV; G.M. Grant, 'President's Address,' T, 1891, S II, XXXI

23 P, 1897, X; P, 1898, XV

24 P, 1882, XXI; Saunders, 'On the Importance of Economizing and Preserving Our Forests,' T, 1882, S IV, 35–7; Macoun, 'The Forests of Canada and Their Distribution,' T, 1894, S IV, 3–20; NA, Robert Bell Papers, Vol. 37, 'A Talk on the Forests of Canada at Rideau Hall,' 29 March 1894; Mair, 'The American Bison,' T, 1890, S III, 93–108; Harvey, 'The Artificial Propagation of Marine Food Fishes and Edible Crustaceans,' T, 1892, S IV, 17–37. The awakening of interest in conservation in this period was expressed in many other quarters, as is illustrated in H.V. Nelles, *The Politics of Development* (Toronto, 1974); Janet Foster, *Working for Wildlife: The Beginnings of Preservation in Canada* (Toronto, 1978); and Michel F. Girard, *L'Écologisme retrouvé: essor et déclin de la Commission de la Conservation du Canada* (Ottawa, 1994).

25 E.E. Prince, 'Marine Biological Stations of Canada,' T, 1907, S IV, 71–92

26 P, 1927, XVIII; Vittorio De Vecchi, 'Science and Government in Nineteenth Century Canada' (PhD thesis, University of Toronto, 1978), 323

27 P, 1904, VIII

28 P, 1887, IV

29 P, 1895, XLI. The character of the natural history societies is discussed in C. Berger, *Science, God, and Nature in Victorian Canada* (Toronto, 1983), chap. 1, and the culture of science in one region is evoked in Paul A. Bogaard, ed., *Profiles of Science and Society in the Maritimes prior to 1914* (Victoria, BC, 1990).

30 P, 1907, Appendix G, CXIV

31 A.S. Eve, 'Modern Views of the Constitution of the Atom,' T, 1914, S III, 10

32 P, 1909, LXII; 1886, XXV

33 NA, Otto J. Klotz Papers, Diary, 15 May 1895 and 19 May 1896

34 R.C. Wallace, 'The Educational Value of the Geological Sciences,' T, 1929, S IV, 3

35 'Colonialism and Literature,' *Sara Jeannette Duncan: Selected Journalism*, ed. T.E. Tausky (Ottawa, 1978), 108

36 P, 1887, XIII. On Bourinot's historical work see C. Berger, 'Race and Liberty: The Historical Ideas of Sir John George Bourinot,' Canadian Historical Association, *Report*, 1965, 87–104, and on imperialism, C. Berger, *The Sense of Power: Studies in the Ideas of Canadian Imperialism, 1867–1914* (Toronto, 1970).

37 P, 1900, II. After admission of Saskatchewan and Alberta as provinces in 1905 this seal became too cluttered and was abandoned.

38 P, 1900, XXXIII–XLIV

Chapter Two History and Ethnology

1 On romantic fiction and history see Carole Gerson, *A Purer Taste: The Writing and Reading of Fiction in English in Nineteenth-Century Canada* (Toronto, 1989).

2 P, 1898, XXXV; 1900, IIII; Gerald Killan, *Preserving Ontario's Heritage: A History of the Ontario Historical Society* (Ottawa, 1976)

3 Hilary B. Neary, 'William Renwick Riddell: Judge, Ontario Publicist and Man of Letters,' *The Law Society of Upper Canada Gazette*, 11 (Sept. 1977), 144–74; Chad Reimer, 'Frederic W. Howay and the Writing of British Columbia History,' paper read to the Canadian Historical Association annual meeting, 22 June 1992

4 P, 1897, XXIV–XXV

5 C.J. Taylor, *Negotiating the Past: The Making of Canada's National Historic Parks and Sites* (Montreal, 1990)

6 Bowman, 'Fundamental Processes in Historical Science,' T, 1912, S II, 133–64 and 489–587; LeSueur, 'History, Its Nature and Methods,' P, 1913, Appendix A, LVII–LXXXIII; Queen's University Archives, Adam Shortt Papers, LeSueur to Shortt, 20 Aug. 1906. LeSueur's problems with publishing

his life of Mackenzie are fully dealt with by A.B. McKillop, *A Critical Spirit: The Thought of William Dawson LeSueur* (Toronto, 1977), and Danielle Hamelin, 'Nurturing Canadian Letters: Four Studies in the Publishing and Promotion of Canadian Literature, 1890–1920' (PhD thesis, University of Toronto, 1994).

7 P, 1924, IV–VII; Serge Gagnon, *Quebec and Its Historians, 1840–1920* (Montreal, 1982), chap. 3.

8 On the controversy over the deportation of the Acadians see M. Brook Taylor, *Promoters, Patriots and Partisans: Historiography in Nineteenth-Century English Canada* (Toronto, 1989), chap. 6.

9 Hector Fabre, 'La Fin de la domination française et l'historien Parkman,' T, 1888, S I, 3–12; P.B. Casgrain, 'A Few Remarks on the "Siege of Quebec,"' T, 1903, S II, 101–33; Louis-Philippe Geoffrion, 'Le Parler des habitants de Québec,' T, 1928, S I, 63–80; J.-L. Olivier Maurault, 'Sur un manuel de l'littérature canadienne,' T, 1935, S I, 77–86

10 Wood, 'An Ursuline Epic,' T, 1908, S II, 3–59; Withrow, 'The Adventures of Isaac Jogues, S.J.,' T, 1885, S II, 45–53, and 'The Jesuit Missions of Canada,' T, 1904, S II, 201–12; Dawson, 'A Plea for Literature,' P, 1908, Appendix A, LXVI

11 Wilson, 'President's Address,' T, 1886, XIV–XX

12 Patterson, 'The Beothiks or Red Indians of Newfoundland,' T, 1891, S II, 123–71; Schultz, 'The Innuits of Our Arctic Coast,' T, 1894, S II, 113–34

13 Hale, 'Language as a Test of Mental Capacity,' T, 1891, S II, 77–112; 'An Iroquois Condoling Ceremony,' T, 1895, S II, 451–65

14 Gail Avrith, 'Science at the Margins: The British Association and the Foundations of Canadian Anthropology, 1884–1910' (PhD thesis, University of Pennsylvania, 1986); Douglas Cole, 'The Origins of Canadian Anthropology, 1850–1910,' *Journal of Canadian Studies*, 8 (1973), 339–460

15 'Traditional History of the Confederacy of the Six Nations,' T, 1911, S II, 195–246

16 Barbeau, 'Le Folklore canadien-français,' T, 1916, S I, 449–81; 'Le pays de Gourganes,' T, 1917, S I, 193–225

Chapter Three The Sciences

1 Bain, 'The International Scientific Catalogue,' *Proceedings of the Royal Canadian Institute*, New Series, II (1878–1903), 27; Morris Zaslow, *Reading the Rocks: The Story of the Geological Survey of Canada, 1842–1972* (Ottawa, 1975)

2 National Museum of Natural Sciences, John Macoun Papers, Letterbook, 1892–3, Macoun to George Lawson, 21 Oct. 1892

3 Mills, 'A Short Chapter in Comparative Physiology and Psychology,' T, 1906, S IV, 300

4 Lawson, 'On the Present State of Botany,' T, 1891, S IV, 17–20

5 Mario Bunge and William R. Shea, eds., *Rutherford and Physics at the Turn of the Century* (New York, 1979)

6 J. Loudon, 'The University in Relation to Research,' T, 1902, Appendix A, XLIX–LIX; Yves Gingras, 'The Institutionalization of Scientific Research in Canada: The Case of Physics,' *Canadian Historical Review*, 67 (June 1986), 181–94

7 A. Stanley Mackenzie, 'The War and Science,' T, 1918, S III, 1–6

8 Alfred Baker, 'Canada's Intellectual Status and Intellectual Needs,' T, 1916, Appendix A, LXIII

9 Macallum, 'The Old Knowledge and the New,' T, 1917, Appendix A, LIX–LXXIII

10 P, 1892, XII

11 T, 1902, S III, 61; W.A.C. McBryde, 'William Lash Miller,' *Journal of Canadian Studies*, 26 (Fall 1991), 101–19

12 P, 1926, XXXIII

13 A.B. McKillop, *Matters of Mind: The University in Ontario, 1791–1951* (Toronto, 1994), 344

14 H.H. Langton, *Sir John Cunningham McLennan: A Memoir* (Toronto, 1939), lists his publications in Appendix II.

15 P, 1927, XXXII; P, 1938, 38

16 P, 1923, XLVIII

17 RSC Papers, Box 29, File 'Reorganization of the RSC-Burpee Correspondence, 1936–37,' Lanctot to Burpee, 18 Dec. 1936

18 Ibid., Boyle to Burpee, 31 Dec. 1936

19 Ibid., Huntsman to Burpee, 22 Dec. 1936

20 P, 1913, XL; RSC Papers, Box I, 'Minutes of Council from 1908 to 1916,' 8 Jan. 1913

21 Marianne G. Ainley, ed., *Despite the Odds: Essays in Canadian Women and Science* (Montreal, 1990); Alison Prentice, 'Blue Stockings, Feminists, or Women Workers? A Preliminary Look at Women's Early Employment at the University of Toronto,' *Journal of the Canadian Historical Association*, 1991, 231–61

22 NA, W.L.M. King Papers, Diary, 24 May 1932

23 P, 1933, XXI

24 P, 1929, VIII

25 J. Playfair McMurrich, 'The Royal Society of Canada: Its Aims and Needs,' T, 1923, Appendix, LV; RSC Papers, Box I, 'Council Meetings, Minutes, 1937–1939,' 18 Feb. 1939

26 P, 1939, 43, 60–4

27 P, 1947, 68

28 RSC Papers, Box 30, File 'Carnegie Grant, 1930–31,' L. Burpee to F.S. Nowlan, 31 Jan. 1931

29 P, 1932, VIII; P, 1943, 30–1

30 RSC Papers, Box 30, File 'Carnegie Grant, 1930–31,' R.W. Brock to Charles Camsell, 22 Sept. 1930

31 Royal Commission on the Arts, Letters and Sciences, *Report* (Ottawa: 1951), 439

Chapter Four Relations between the Humanities
and the Sciences

1 Ganong, 'A Monograph on the Place-nomenclature of the Province of New Brunswick,' T, 1896, S II, 176; 'A Monograph on the Cartography of the Province of New Brunswick,' T, 1897, S II, 314

2 P, 1942, Appendix B, 91–2

3 Wilson, 'President's Address,' P, 1886, XIV–XX

4 Hamel, 'President's Address,' P, 1887, XIV–XXII; T, 1891, S III, 3–7; P, 1890, XIX

5 C. Holland, *William Dawson LeSueur (1840–1917): A Canadian Man of Letters* (San Francisco, 1993), 36–7

6 H.B. Macallum, 'The Semi-Centennial of the Origin of

Species,' T, 1909, S IV, 177–90; Ramsay Wright, 'The Progress of Biology,' T, 1911, XXXVII–XLVIII

7 Parks, 'Time and Life,' P, 1926, LXVII–LXXXV
8 Dawson, 'A Plea for Literature,' P, 1908, Appendix A, LV–LVI
9 Hutton, 'Thucydides and History,' T, 1916, S II, 225–46. On Hutton and his contemporaries, see S.E.D. Shortt, *In Search of an Ideal: Six Canadian Intellectuals and Their Convictions in an Age of Transition, 1890–1930* (Toronto, 1976); Alan F. Bowker, '"Truly Useful Men": Maurice Hutton, George Wrong, James Mavor and the University of Toronto, 1880–1927' (PhD thesis, University of Toronto, 1975); A.B. McKillop, *Matters of Mind: The University in Ontario, 1791–1951* (Toronto, 1994)
10 Falconer, 'The Conflict of Educational Ideals arising out of the Present War,' T, 1918, S II, 227–40
11 Maurice Lebel, 'Bibliographie des mémoires relatifs à l'antiquité classique présentés a la Société royale du Canada,' T, 1963, 68; W.H. Alexander, 'The Classical Discipline in Education, 1899–1939,' T, 1939, S II, 9–21
12 P.G.C. Campbell, 'A University Forty Years Ago,' *Queen's Quarterly*, 48 (Autumn 1941), 251; P, 1940, Appendix C, 98
13 Leacock, *Arcadian Adventures with the Idle Rich* (Toronto, 1959), 39–40
14 G.M. Grant, 'President's Address,' T, 1891, XXXIV
15 Scott, 'Poetry and Progress,' P, 1922, Appendix A, XLXXII–LXVII
16 Edgar, 'Are Our Writers in the Modern Stream?,' T, 1927, S II, 1–6. Years later Scott said that he never did get on very far with Joyce's *Ulysses*. 'I smuggled one of the first copies into Canada from France when it was thought daring to even mention the work, and it's around here somewhere in seclusion if not in hiding, but I will not meddle with it.' NA, E.K. Brown Papers, Scott to Brown, 5–6 March 1945
17 Stewart, 'Tolstoy as a Problem in Psycho-Analysis,' T, 1923, S II, 29–39; 'The Declining Fame of Thomas Carlyle,' T, 1920, S II, 39–46
18 Brett, 'The Revolt against Reason,' T, 1919, S II, 9–17; 'The

History of Science as a Factor in Modern Education,'
T, 1925, S II, 39–46

19 Tory, 'A Study of the Organization and Work of the Royal
Society of Canada,' T, 1940, 65

Chapter Five The Rise of the Social Sciences

1 Gérin, 'L'Habitant de Saint-Justin,' T, 1898, S I, 139–216;
'Nôtre Mouvement intellectuel,' T, 1901, S I, 145–72; 'Le
Vulgarisation de la science sociale chez les Canadiens
français,' T, 1905, S I, 67–87; 'La Sociologie : le mot et la
chose,' T, 1915, S I, 321–56. That Gérin was not alone in
responding to French sociology is clear in Pierre Trépanier,
'Les Influences leplaysiennes au Canada français, 1855–
1888,' *Journal of Canadian Studies*, 22 (Spring 1987), 66–83.

2 Bouchette, 'L'Evolution économique dans la Province de
Québec,' T, 1901, S I, 117–44; Montpetit, 'Introduction à
l'étude de l'économie politique,' T, 1916, S I, 365–408

3 P, 1941, 47

4 Bourinot, 'The Study of Political Science in Canadian
Universities,' T, 1889, S II, 3–16; *Papers and Proceedings of the
Canadian Political Science Association, 1913* (Ottawa, 1913), 5;
Barry Ferguson, *Remaking Liberalism: The Intellectual Legacy
of Adam Shortt, O.D. Skelton, W.C. Clark, and W.A. Mackin-
tosh, 1890–1925* (Montreal, 1993)

5 Marlene Shore, *The Science of Social Redemption: McGill, the
Chicago School, and the Origins of Social Research in Canada*
(Toronto, 1987)

6 Leacock, 'The Economic Aspect of Aviation,' T, 1928, S II,
213–32; P, 1944, 106. On Leacock's attitude to economics see
C. Berger, 'The Other Mr. Leacock,' *Canadian Literature*, 55
(Winter 1973), 23–40

7 B. Ferguson and D. Owram, 'Social Scientists and Public
Policy from the 1920s through World War II,' *Journal of
Canadian Studies* (Winter 1980–1), 4

8 J.A.B. McLeish, *A Canadian for All Seasons: The John E.*

Robbins Story (Toronto, 1978), chaps. 7–8; Watson Kirkconnell, *A Slice of Canada: Memoirs* (Toronto, 1967)

9 On the nationalist and reformist network see Doug Owram, *The Government Generation: Canadian Intellectuals and the State, 1900–1945* (Toronto, 1986); Mary Vipond, 'The Nationalist Network: English Canada's Intellectuals and Artists in the 1920's,' in J.M. Bumsted, ed., *Interpreting Canada's Past*, Vol. 2, *After Confederation* (Toronto, 1986), 261–77

10 RSC Papers, Box I, 'Council Meetings, 1917–1939,' 3 Dec. 1938; Lawrence D. Stokes, 'Canada and an Academic Refugee from Germany: The Case of Gerhard Herzberg,' *Canadian Historical Review*, 57 (June 1976), 150–70

11 Ibid., Box 28, File 'Reorganization of the RSC ... ,' Innis to Burpee, 23 Dec. 1936. On Innis and the social sciences see C. Berger, *The Writing of Canadian History* (Toronto, 1976); Ian Drummond, *Political Economy at the University of Toronto: A History of the Department, 1888–1982* (Toronto, 1991); A.B. McKillop, *Matters of Mind: The University in Ontario, 1791–1951* (Toronto, 1994).

12 Queen's University Archives, A.R.M. Lower Papers, Innis to Lower, 15 Nov. 1939

13 H.M. Tory, 'A Study of the Organization and Work of the Royal Society of Canada,' T, 1940, 67

14 P, 1940, 67; P, 1941, 43; RSC Papers, Box 50, 'Minute Book of Section II from May, 1911 to June, 1942,' 20 May 1941

15 R. Harris, *A History of Higher Education in Canada, 1663–1960* (Toronto, 1976), 438

16 Jean-Charles Falardeau, 'Léon Gérin,' in Laurier Lapierre, ed., *Four o'Clock Lectures: French-Canadian Thinkers of the Nineteenth and Twentieth Centuries* (Montreal, 1966), 159

Chapter Six French-English Relations to Mid-Century

1 Dawson, 'A Plea for Literature,' P, 1908, Appendix A, LI. Chauveau's comment was brought to my attention by Donald Smith of the University of Calgary.

2 Grant, 'President's Address,' T, 1891, S II, XXXIII; Alexander Johnson, 'Our Semi-Jubilee and Canada,' P, 1906, Appendix A, XLII

3 Jean Bruchési, 'Culture in Canada,' T, 1951, 151

4 P, 1915, S I, XXXIII–XXXIV; P, 1915, XLIV

5 Routhier, 'Le Dualisme canadien,' P, 1915, Appendix A, XLIX–LVII; Bégin, 'Relations de l'église et l'état,' T, 1915, S I, 165–71; Paquet, 'La Notion du droit,' T, 1915, S I, 129–43; Lemieux, 'Le Canada, la guerre et demain,' P, 1919, Appendix A, XLVII–LI

6 Bruchési, 'Le Problème des races au Canada,' T, 1915, S I, 5–11; P, 1916, XXIII

7 On Marie-Victorin and the Royal Society, see L. Chartrand, Raymond Duchesne, and Yves Gingras, Histoire des sciences au Québec (Montreal, 1987), 311–12.

8 P, 1952, Appendix B, 73

9 Napoléon Legendre, 'La Femme dans société moderne,' T, 1890, S I, 13–24; Joseph Royal, 'Le Socialisme au États-Unis et au Canada,' T, 1894, S I, 49–61

10 According to Fernand Ouellet, 'Among Quebec Francophone authors of articles of an historical nature in the transactions of this association from 1882 to 1941, the proportion of clerics rose from 37 percent between 1882 and 1901 to 59 percent during the years from 1922 to 1941.' The Socialization of Quebec Historiography since 1960 (Toronto, 1988), 7

11 Paquet, 'La Philosophie et l'histoire et Bossuet,' T, 1928, S I, 23–35; Robert, 'La Morale et la sociologie,' T, 1922, S I, 91–108; Paquet, 'Dieu dans la civilisation canadienne,' T, 1934, S I, LXXVII; Emard, 'Le Canada à Rome au Jubilé de 1925,' T, 1926, S I, 1–16; Auclair, 'La Canadienne française,' T, 1936, S I, 80

12 Chartier, 'La Vie de l'esprit au Canada français,' T, 1939, S I, 43; T, 1934, S I, 105

13 Lanctot, 'Influences américaines dans le Québec,' T, 1937, S I, 119–25

14 Chartier, 'L'Ecole régionaliste au Canada français (1820–1920),' T, 1928, S I, 20

15 Roy, 'Provincialisme intellectuel au Canada,' T, 1929, Appendix A, XXXIII–XLVII
16 I owe this information to Andrée Désilets.
17 Lebel, 'Apport de la Société royale du Canada à la vie intellectuelle du pays ... (1882–1978),' T, 1979, 3–15
18 P, 1938, Appendix C, 106–7
19 Groulx, *Mes Mémoires* (Montreal, 1970), tome I, 311–14
20 Wade, *The French Canadians, 1760–1945* (Toronto, 1956), 1077
21 P, 1948, 50
22 Jean Lamarre, *Le Devenir de la Nation québécoise selon Maurice Séguin, Guy Frégault et Michel Brunet, 1944–1969* (Sillery [Quebec], 1993)

Chapter Seven Postwar Malaise

1 Huntsman, 'President's Address,' P, 1938, 23–7
2 Brebner, *Scholarship in Canada* (Ottawa, 1945), 65–6
3 'Résumé of the Memorial of the Royal Society of Canada to the Massey Commission,' P, 1950, Appendix D, 171–2; Paul Litt, *The Muses, the Masses and the Massey Commission* (Toronto, 1992)
4 RSC Papers, Box 22, 'Draft of a brief concerning research in the humanities, for presentation by the Royal Society of Canada to the Senate Committee on science policy,' 16 Oct. 1968, 1–2
5 Box 30, Léon Lortie to Jean Boûcher, 25 Feb. 1969
6 P, 1948, 33
7 Bruchési, 'Culture in Canada,' T, 1951, 141–57
8 Lower, 'The Canadian University,' T, 1953, 16
9 Morton, 'The "North" in Canadian Historiography,' T, 1970, 31–40; Pacey, '"Summer's Heat and Winter's Frigid Gales': The Effects of Climate on Canadian Literature,' Ibid., 3–23; Keenleyside, 'The Human Resources and Problems of the Canadian North,' T, 1950, Appendix B, 143. These remarks remind one of an apparently serious com-

ment made by Sir James Grant, physician to a succession of governors general, in his presidential address of 1903;   'Colder climates appear to favour large brains, which may in a measure account for the marked intellectual activity of our Canadian people. The tables of average brain weights of various nationalities ... produce evidence of greater brain weights in colder climates. As proof of such, it is known that the colder air of the United States, produces larger brains in the negroes than the warm air of South Africa.' P, 1903, Appendix A, LIV–LV

10 J.W.T. Spinks, 'The Natural Sciences,' *Royal Commission Studies: A Selection of Essays Prepared for the Royal Commission on National Development in the Arts, Letters and Sciences* (Ottawa, 1951), 272

11 RSC Papers, Box 1, Minutes of Council, 19 Feb. 1949, 'Report from Section III on Reorganization of the Society'

12 Ibid., File 'Council Meeting Minutes, 1952–74,' Herzberg to W.H. Cook, 1 Oct. 1952

13 M.Y. Williams, 'The Earth Sciences and the Royal Society of Canada,' T, 1961, 65

14 T, 1955, 46; RSC papers, Box 1, File 'Council Meeting Minutes 1955–59,' 'Report to the Council of the Society on Publications Policy. Prepared by the Publications Committee for the Meeting of February 18th, 1956'

15 T, 1960, 50

16 Scott, 'The Place of the Academy in the Modern World,' T, 1963, 16–24

17 T, 1965, 67

18 Dolman, 'St. Elmo's and St. Anthony's Fires,' T, 1970, 31–51

19 J.H. Chapman, 'The Royal Society of Canada: What Is It?,' T, 1973, 263–73

20 RSC Papers, Box 50, File 'Woodcock, George,' Woodcock to E.T. Salmon, 8 April 1975; *At the Mermaid Inn: Wilfred Campbell, Archibald Lampman, Duncan Campbell Scott in the Globe 1892–93*, Introduction by Barrie Davies (Toronto, 1979), 338

Chapter Eight Three Decades of Reform

1 This brief is in RSC Papers, Box 22. P, 1964, 55; P, 1965, 44
2 Bruchési, 'Regards sur la Société Royale de Canada ...,'
  T, 1954, 54
3 T, 1961, 56
4 John Porter, *The Vertical Mosaic* (Toronto, 1965), 504–5; R.O.
  Ogmundson and J. McLauglin, 'Changes in the Intellectual
  Elite, 1960–1990: The Royal Society Revisited,' *Canadian
  Review of Sociology and Anthropology*, 31, no. 1 (Feb 1994),
  1–13
5 Lortie, 'Grandeur et servitude des arts et des sciences,'
  T, 1969, 1–16
6 RSC Papers, Box 46, File 'Candidatures, 1964'
7 Lebel, 'Le Rôle des humanités dans une ère technologique,'
  T, 1969, 31; Patricia Jasen, '"In Pursuit of Human Values (or
  Laugh When You Say That)": The Student Critique of the
  Arts Curriculum in the 1960s,' in Paul Axelrod and John G.
  Reid, eds., *Youth, University and Canadian Society: Essays
  in the Social History of Higher Education* (Montreal, 1989),
  247–71
8 Science Council of Canada, *Social Science Research in Canada*
  (Ottawa, 1985), 51
9 RSC Papers, Box 50, File 'Academy II, 1973–78,' S.D. Clark,
  'Why the Royal Society of Canada Is in Trouble: The Case
  of the Social Sciences,' 1–2
10 Lamontagne, 'The Scientist and the Politician,' T, 1969,
   49–55
11 Smith, 'The Social Sciences and the "Economics of Research,"' T, 1968, 21–33
12 H.R. Wynne-Edwards, 'A Review of the Current Status of
   Science Policy in Canada,' T, 1969, 303–12; W.A. Douglas,
   'Towards a National Science Policy, or Away,' T, 1969,
   297–301
13 Herzberg, 'Remarks on the Boundaries of Knowledge,'
   T, 1974, 28–9

14 B.S. Kierstead and S.D. Clark, 'The Social Sciences,' *Royal Commission Studies: A Selection of Essays Prepared for the Royal Commission on National Development in the Arts, Letters and Sciences* (Ottawa, 1951), 185

15 RSC Papers, Box 22, 'Brief to the Special Senate Committee on Science Policy,' 1969

16 Mario Bunge, 'The Popular Perception of Science in North America,' T, 1989, 269–80

17 T, 1987, 25

18 T, 1989, 63–5

19 Royal Society of Canada, Development Plan, 1993

20 E.W.R. Steacie, 'Science and the National Academy,' T, 1955, 55; ARA Consulting Group, Final Report. Evaluation of Industry Canada's Support to the Royal Society of Canada, Dec. 1993

21 T, 1990, 29

22 T, 1986, 41

23 Porter, *Vertical Mosaic*, 503

Chapter Nine Reflections

1 Brebner, *Canada: A Modern History* (Ann Arbor, Mich., 1960), 302

2 James G. Greenlee, *Sir Robert Falconer: A Biography* (Toronto, 1988); W.A. Waiser, *The Field Naturalist: John Macoun, the Geological Survey, and Natural Science* (Toronto, 1989); M. Christine King, *E.W.R. Steacie and Science in Canada* (Toronto, 1989); David G. Pitt, *E.J. Pratt: The Master Years, 1927–1964* (Toronto, 1987)

3 Robin S. Harris, *A History of Higher Education in Canada, 1663–1960* (Toronto, 1976), 602

4 R.O. Ogmundson and J.M. McLauglin, 'Changes in the Intellectual Elite, 1960–1990: The Royal Society Revisited,' *Canadian Review of Sociology and Anthropology*, 31, no. 1 (Feb. 1994), 1–13

5 Lower, *My First Seventy-five Years* (Toronto, 1967), 372

6 William Christian, *George Grant: A Biography* (Toronto, 1993), 298, 429 n. 33
7 P, 1936, XXIII

Index